HUMAN RIGHTS
Questions and Answers

4527

H U M A N
R I G H T S
Questions and Answers

Leah Levin
Illustrated by Plantu

UNESCO PUBLISHING

First published in 1981 by the United Nations Educational,
Scientific and Cultural Organization,
7, place de Fontenoy, 75352 Paris 07 SP

Reprinted with corrections, 1982
Second edition, updated, 1989
Third edition, 1996
Fourth edition, updated, 2004
Fifth edition, updated, 2009

The previous editions have been translated into the following languages: English, 1981, 1982, 1989, 1996, 1998, 2004; French, 1981, 1996, 2005; Spanish, 1982, 1999; Finnish, 1983, 2003; German, 1983; Greek, 1985; Portuguese, 1985; Swedish, 1985, 2000; Arabic, 1986; Danish, 1986; Indonesian, 1987; Japanese, 1988, 1999; Slovak, 1993; Russian, 1993, 1997; Armenian, 1994, 1998; Belarusian, 1995; Bulgarian, 1997; Georgian, 1997; Urdu, 1998; Assamiya, 1998; Bangala, 1998; Hindi, 1998; Kannada, 1998; Marathi, 1998; Tamil, 1998; Romanian, 1998, 2002; Esperanto, 1998; Azerbaijani, 1999; Spanish/Basque 1999; Basque, 2000; Bosnian, 2001; Albanian, 2001; Mongolian, 2005

© UNESCO
All rights reserved
ISBN UNESCO 978-92-3-104130-3

The authors are responsible for the choice and the presentation of the facts contained in this book and for the opinions expressed therein, which are not necessarily those of UNESCO and do not commit the Organization.

The designations employed and the presentation of material throughout this publication do not imply the expression of any opinion whatsoever on the part of UNESCO concerning the legal status of any country, territory, city or area or of its authorities, or concerning the delimitation of its frontiers or boundaries.

Typeset by Jacqueline Gensollen-Bloch
Printed by Jouve, Mayenne

Printed in France

Preface

When the United Nations was created in 1945, the founding States reaffirmed their faith in fundamental human rights, in the dignity and worth of the human person and in the equal rights of men and women. They expressed their determination to create a world where human rights and fundamental freedoms would be universally respected and observed for all without distinction as to race, sex, language or religion.

The Universal Declaration of Human Rights, adopted in 1948, was the embodiment of this determination. For the first time in history, fundamental rights and freedoms of all members of the human family were internationally agreed upon. The provisions of the Universal Declaration were acknowledged as a common standard of achievement for all peoples and all nations. They became a source of inspiration for constitutions and national laws of a great number of States. The Universal Declaration, translated into more than 350 languages, is the most well known normative human rights instrument.

The rights enshrined in the Universal Declaration were further elaborated and became universally binding standards through the adoption in 1966 of the International Covenant on Civil and Political Rights and the International Covenant on Economic, Social and Cultural Rights. Other treaties, including the International Convention on the Elimination of All Forms of Racial Discrimination, the Convention on the Elimination of All Forms of Discrimination against Women, the Convention on the Rights of the Child, the Convention Against Torture, the International Convention on the Protection of the Rights of all Migrant Workers and Members of their Families, the Convention on the Rights of Persons with Disabilities and the International Convention for the Protection of All Persons from Enforced Disappearance established new standards and enlarged the scope of human rights law. All these treaties provide for the creation of mechanisms to monitor whether or not States comply with their obligations. This includes the submission of regular reports on the measures States are taking to implement the provisions of the treaties. In certain cases, there is also the possibility for individuals to file a complaint against a State if they feel that their rights have been violated. Other universal and regional instruments (conventions, declarations, recommendations and resolutions) have been adopted to further promote and protect human rights.

Numerous bodies, programmes and specialized agencies within the United Nations system work for the advancement of human rights. For example, the United Nations Children's Fund (UNICEF) defends the rights of the child and the International Labour Organization (ILO) protects the rights of workers. The United Nations Educational, Scientific and Cultural Organization (UNESCO) contributes 'to peace and security by promoting collaboration among the nations through education, science and culture in order to further universal respect for justice, for the rule of law and for the human rights and fundamental freedoms'.

UNESCO is particularly involved in the promotion of the right to education, the right to freedom of opinion and expression, the right to take part in cultural life and the right to enjoy the benefits of scientific progress and its applications. In October 2003, UNESCO adopted a Strategy on Human Rights and an Integrated Strategy to Combat Racism, Discrimination, Xenophobia and Related Intolerance. These closely interlinked strategies reaffirm the human rights mandate of UNESCO and aim at the reinforcement of the Organization's contribution to the promotion and protection of human rights and the struggle against old and new forms of discrimination. Research and dissemination of knowledge are the main actions through which the aims of the two strategies are to be achieved. UNESCO works in close cooperation with the Office of the United Nations High Commissioner for Human Rights (OHCHR) which coordinates human rights activities within the United Nations system.

Many other intergovernmental organizations are active in the field of human rights. Such regional organizations as the African Union, the Council of Europe, the Organization for Security and Co-operation in Europe and the Organization of American States, successfully working for the advancement of human rights, should be mentioned.

At the Millennium Summit (United Nations, New York, 6–8 September 2000), States recognized human rights as the indispensable foundation of a more peaceful, prosperous and just world and reaffirmed their collective responsibility to uphold human rights at the global level. They committed themselves to create a shared future for all the people of the world, based upon common humanity in all its diversity. The United Nations Millennium Declaration adopted at the Summit sets forth concrete goals to guide and encourage governments in their efforts to bring about globalization with a human face.

The creation in 2006 of the Human Rights Council and the introduction of the Universal Periodic Review (UPR) of States' compliance with their human rights obligations opened a new page in the struggle for human rights. The Human Rights Council gives great importance to the promotion of human rights education. To this end, it has enabled the Human Rights Council Advisory Committee to prepare a draft declaration on human rights education and training (Human Rights Council Resolution A/HRC/6/10 of 28 September 2007). UNESCO is actively involved in the process of the drafting of the declaration.

While States preserve the primary responsibility for establishing human rights standards and ensuring their implementation, other actors are becoming increasingly influential in the promotion and protection of human rights. Thousands of non-governmental organizations are actively involved in the promotion and protection of human rights. They are acting as 'watchdogs' in case of non-implementation of existing human rights instruments and as catalysts of the progressive development of human rights law. The academic community, media and the business world need to work together with governments, State institutions, intergovernmental and non-governmental organizations to achieve the aims proclaimed in the United Nations Charter, the UNESCO Constitution and the Universal Declaration of Human Rights.

Thanks to the efforts of the international community and human rights activists, the protection of human rights has substantially improved in the last decades. Respect for human dignity and non-discrimination, which imply equal rights and opportunities for all, are now being instilled in the minds of people. Human rights have become an integral part of the international and national political agenda along with the growing conviction that human rights violations still occurring in various parts of the world should not go unpunished.

However, despite indisputable achievements, the state of implementation of human rights standards in the world is still far from satisfactory. Sixty years after the adoption of the Universal Declaration of Human Rights many millions of children, especially girls, have no access to education, decent housing continues to be just a dream for hundreds of millions of families, and the right to health and the right to food are not ensured properly for almost one third of the world population. Lack of access to safe drinking water and sanitation takes a heavy toll on human rights in a number of countries.

Despite all these efforts at national and international levels, discrimination and gender inequality persist. While widespread poverty continues to be the major obstacle to the attainment of all human rights for all, other threats and dangers, such as terrorism, organized crime, corruption, deterioration of the environment and climate change, challenge the progress in the advancement of human rights.

The current global economic and financial crises have produced a serious negative impact on the implementation of human rights in the world. They have led to the dramatic rise of unemployment, which can further lead to the rise of xenophobia and discrimination, in particular with regard to migrant workers. Further aggravation of the food crisis, and decline in foreign investments and development aid are other consequences. The crises can seriously impede the attainment of the Millennium Development Goals and undermine the fundamental principle applied to economic, social and cultural rights – the principle of non-retrogression.

ILO estimates that, as a result of the crisis, global unemployment in 2009 could increase, in comparison with 2007, by 18 to 30 million and even by 50 million, if the situation continues to deteriorate (see *Global Employment Trends Report 2009*, ILO-January 2009, p.19).[1]

Alarmed by the current situation, in February 2009 the Human Rights Council convened a special session and adopted a resolution entitled 'The Impact of the Global Economic and Financial Crises on the Universal Realization and Effective Enjoyment of Human Rights' (A/HRC/S-10/L.1, 23 February 2009). In the Resolution, the Council addressed its serious concern about the negative impact of the multiple and interrelated global crises on economic and social development and on the full enjoyment of all human rights in all countries. It recognized that developing countries are in a more vulnerable position. The Council called upon States to note that the crises do not diminish the responsibility of national authorities and the international community in the realization of human rights. The Council urged that special attention in these hard times be paid to non-discrimination and to the ways and means of ensuring respect for and protection of the rights of the disadvantaged and marginalized groups, women, children, migrants, migrant workers and members of their families, indigenous peoples and people living in poverty.

The General Assembly of the United Nations held in June 2009 a High-Level Conference on the world economic and financial crisis and its impact on development. Its aim was to identify emergency and long-term responses to mitigate the impact of the crisis, especially on vulnerable groups. The report of the UN High Commissioner for Human Rights with suggested recommendations on overcoming the negative consequences of the crisis on human rights was a major contribution to the discussions. The meeting culminated with the approval of an outcome document. Inter alia, the General Assembly was asked to follow up, through an ad hoc open-ended working group, on a number of issues such as crisis mitigation, the restructuring of the financial and economic system and architecture, external debt, and international trade.

---

*   See Endnotes at the end of this book.

Challenges and obstacles to the implementation of human rights require a profound analysis. To find sustainable solutions to existing and emerging problems, an increased awareness on the part of all actors is indispensable. Human rights education is a vehicle to sensitize society at large on human rights issues and to create an environment conducive to the implementation of human rights and to the prevention of human rights violations. People can only enjoy their rights and fight for their implementation if they have sufficient knowledge about the content of human rights and procedures to defend them. Human rights education should promote fundamental principles such as the equal importance of all human rights – civil, cultural, economic, political and social – for the dignity and well-being of everyone. It should also raise awareness on old and new threats to human rights. Human rights education is not limited to training and dissemination of information. Its overarching aim is to build a universal culture of human rights, which implies knowledge and skills, as well as behavioural patterns, based upon the universal principles of justice, the rule of law and non-discrimination.

• • •

Human Rights: Questions and Answers responds to the growing interest of the general public in human rights issues. Written by Leah Levin, a distinguished British human rights specialist, it provides ample information on human rights. The previous editions (the first of which appeared in 1981) have proven to be a valuable teaching aid on human rights and have been translated into more than 30 languages. This new edition, while maintaining the original structure, has been substantially enlarged, revised and recently updated. The first part of the book presents an overview of the scope and content of international human rights law, procedures to monitor its implementation, organizations and institutions working for human rights, major international events, as well as new developments and challenges. The second part clarifies the meaning of the different articles of the Universal Declaration of Human Rights. Plantu, a well-known French political cartoonist and devoted human rights partisan, has illustrated all editions of the book, lending the force of image to the cause of human rights.

We wish to thank the author and the artist, as well as all our colleagues, inside and outside the Organization, who contributed to the preparation of this publication.

The work was updated by the Human Rights and Gender Equality Section in May 2009. We wish to express our deep gratitude to Ms Sofia Mamoucha for her precious assistance.

The publication of this teaching aid is part of the International Year of Human Rights Learning, which began in December 2008 on the occasion of the 60th Anniversary of the Universal Declaration of Human Rights. The momentum gained in 2008, during the year-long campaign to commemorate the anniversary in which UNESCO took an active part, must not be lost and efforts to ensure the enjoyment of all human rights by all should be further continued and increased.

Vladimir Volodin
Konstantinos Tararas
Division of Human Rights,
Human Security and Philosophy
Social and Human Sciences Sector
UNESCO

Contents

Author
and Illustrator

Leah Levin is a well-known human rights specialist, author of many articles on child labour and human rights, and active member of several human rights NGOs, both national and international.

She worked for many years as consultant with the then Human Rights Committee of the United Nations Association – United Kingdom, Anti-Slavery International, the International Labour Organization and the University of Essex. From 1982 to 1992, she was director of JUSTICE, the British Section of the International Commission of Jurists. She is currently a member of the Editorial Board of the International Journal of Human Rights and honorary member of the Council of JUSTICE.

In 1992 Levin was awarded a doctorate by the University of Essex and in December 2002, she was awarded the Order of the British Empire (OBE) for her services to international human rights.

Her cooperation with UNESCO dates back to the 1970s. Between 1975 and 1985 she participated in UNESCO human rights education programmes and from 1980 to 1985 contributed to its work as member of the United Kingdom National Commission for UNESCO. The book *Human Rights: Questions and Answers*, first published in 1981, is the most eloquent example of this fruitful cooperation.

Plantu is a distinguished French political cartoonist renowned for his sensitivity to human rights, an issue to which he has dedicated many of his drawings. Plantu has collaborated with several newspapers, including *Le Monde* and *Le Monde Diplomatique*, *Phosphore* and the weekly *L'Express*. In *Le Monde*, he began on 1 October 1972 with a cartoon targeting the war in Viet Nam, and since 1985 a Plantu cartoon has appeared on the first page of each daily edition. In 2002, Plantu celebrated 30 years with *Le Monde* and the publication of over 15,000 cartoons.

The work of Plantu has been presented in numerous exhibitions in France as well as in other countries worldwide, including Argentina, Brazil, Côte d'Ivoire, Iran, Japan, Poland, Sri Lanka and Turkey; the most recent being an exhibition of drawings and sculptures at the Yves Brayer Museum in France (2008). In October 2006, Plantu created with Kofi Annan, in New York, the 'Cartooning for Peace' foundation. It unites cartoonists from all continents in order to encourage people, and notably the media, to 'unlearn intolerance'.[2]

Plantu has received several awards in recognition of his work, including the Mumm Prize for his cartoon 'Gordji chez le juge' in 1988, the *Prix de l'humour noir* in 1989, and the Gat Perich Prize in 1996 (the International Prize for Caricature).

Besides illustrating *Human Rights: Questions and Answers*, he has also illustrated another well-known UNESCO publication, *Introducing Democracy: 80 Questions and Answers*, by David Beetham and Kevin Boyle. Both books have been translated into some thirty languages.

Acknowledgements

The publication of *Human Rights: Questions and Answers* in 1981 by UNESCO aimed to meet the need for human rights teaching material for both the general public and students, as well as activists and non-governmental organizations working for the promotion of human rights.

The idea originated in the watershed UNESCO International Congress on the Teaching of Human Rights, held in Vienna in September 1978, a Recommendation of which was the development of projects related to the teaching of human rights.

This first publication was very much a collaborative effort. It involved several well-known human rights activists including the late Martin Ennals, the late Paul Sieghart, Nigel Rodley and Brian Wrobel. I worked together with them and had the active support and guidance of UNESCO, and in particular Stephen Marks, who recruited Plantu, the power of whose cartoons added the force of image to the text. But for the encouragement and enthusiasm of all those involved, this book might never have seen the light of day.

Since then it has been steadily elaborated to take into account new developments in the field of human rights, with three further editions published in 1989, 1996 and 2004 respectively. To date, it has appeared in over thirty languages.

Grateful thanks are due to the Office of the United Nations High Commissioner for Human Rights (OHCHR). I have had unrestricted access to the various sectors of expertise within the

OHCHR and the valuable help and guidance that I received ensured the accuracy of the relevant texts. My gratitude is also due to the many United Nations agencies and international organizations that provided me with material and contributed to the preparation of the manuscript.

There are many who walked with me part or most of the way, and I cannot mention them all. But among those who have given me their support from the very beginning, I would like to thank Kevin Boyle of the Human Rights Centre, University of Essex, Lee Swepston of the International Labour Organization and John Packer.

Finally, I would like to thank UNESCO for the support and confidence they have placed in me, in particular Vladimir Volodin with whom I have worked in the preparation of the latest editions, and also Konstantinos Tararas and all of the Division of Human Rights who have contributed substantive and fresh ideas to the content of the manuscript as well as to the arrangement of the material.

Leah Levin

Part I

International Human Rights Law: Questions and answers

Human rights: general introduction

1. What is meant by 'human rights'?

Human beings are born equal in dignity and rights. These are moral claims that are inalienable and inherent in all human individuals by virtue of their humanity alone. These claims are articulated and formulated in what today we call human rights, and have been translated into legal rights, established according to the law-creating processes of societies, both on the national and international level. The basis of these legal rights is the consent of the governed, that is the consent of the subjects of the rights.

2. Are human rights accepted universally?

The values of dignity and equality of all members of the human race, like many other basic principles which underlie what today we call human rights, can be found in virtually every culture and civilization, religion and philosophical tradition.[3] Nevertheless, the

---

*   See Endnotes at the end of this book.

idea of rules common to all citizens dates back many centuries. No tradition denies the existence of a fundamental human well-being, the flourishing of which requires respect for the most important needs. Some dispute, however, what this means in practice. Human rights are nevertheless a way of establishing a minimal understanding of what human well-being means, and thereby draw a line that the disputes should not cross. No dispute should justify the loss of innocent lives, make rape acceptable, or allow a government to starve its population. No disagreement can justify the disappearance of those with whom we disagree.

3. How did the idea of human rights protection develop?

The idea that the rights of human beings should be elaborated and protected has been gradually transformed into written norms. Many important landmarks led the way, such as, in England, the Magna Carta (1215), the Petition of Right (1628) and the Bill of Rights (1689). During the eighteenth century, the early ideas of natural law developed into an acceptance of natural rights as legal rights, and these rights for the first time were written into national constitutions. This reflected an almost contractual relationship between the State and the individual, which emphasized that the power of the State derived from the assent of the free individual. The French Declaration of the Rights of Man and of the Citizen of 1789 and the American Bill of Rights of 1791 were based on this premise. During the nineteenth century this principle was adopted by a number of independent States and social and economic rights also began to be recognized. Despite the recognition accorded to human rights in national constitutions, these rights were sometimes curtailed or eliminated by legislation or by arbitrary means and, perhaps generally, by informal social mechanisms. Moreover, human rights, in spite of their status as legal rights, were often violated by States themselves.

4. What were the first steps taken to protect human rights at the international level?

The first international treaties concerning human rights were linked with the acceptance of freedom of religion (e.g. the Treaty of Westphalia of 1648) and the abolition of slavery. Slavery had already been condemned by the Congress of Vienna in 1815 and a number of international treaties on the abolition of slavery emerged in the second half of the nineteenth century (e.g. the Treaty of Washington of 1862 and documents of the conferences in Brussels in 1867 and 1890, and in Berlin in 1885). Another area of international cooperation concerned the development of laws pertaining to the conduct of war (e.g. the Declaration of Paris of 1856, the First Geneva Convention of 1864 and the Second of 1906, and the Hague Conventions of 1899 and 1907). The creation of the International Committee of the Red Cross (ICRC) in 1864 contributed greatly to these developments.[4]

Since the end of the First World War, there has been a growing belief that governments alone cannot safeguard human rights, and that these require international guarantees. Though the mandate of the League of Nations, the first universal intergovernmental organization created after the First World War, did not mention human rights, the League tried to undertake the protection of human rights through international means. However, its concerns were limited mainly to the establishment of certain conditions for the protection of minorities in a few countries.

The standards determining the conditions of industrial workers, established at the beginning of the twentieth century, became the subject of further international agreements elaborated by the International Labour Organization (ILO), created in 1919. The International Slavery Convention, signed in Geneva on 25 September 1926, was the culmination of lengthy efforts aimed at the abolition of slavery. Relevant conventions for the protection of refugees were adopted in 1933 and 1938. However, despite all these developments, human rights law did not emerge in the period between the two world wars.

The totalitarian regimes, established in the 1920s and 1930s, grossly violated human rights in their own territories and subsequently during the Second World War in occupied territories. There was massive abuse of human life and dignity, including the elimination of entire groups of people because of their race, religion or nationality. The experience of the war led to a growing conviction that effective international protection of human rights was one of the essential conditions of international world peace and progress.

5. How is the idea of international human rights protection reflected in the Charter of the United Nations?

The importance of human rights was reflected in and reinforced by the Charter of the United Nations, signed on 26 June 1945. The Charter states the fundamental objectives of the universal organization, namely: 'to save succeeding generations from the scourge of war' and 'to reaffirm faith in fundamental human rights, in the dignity and worth of the human person and in the equal rights of men and women'. Article 1 of the Charter states that one of the aims of the United Nations is to achieve international cooperation in 'promoting and encouraging respect for human rights and for fundamental freedoms for all without distinction as to race, sex, language or religion', thus enshrining the principle of non-discrimination. Article 55 expresses a similar aim, and by Article 56 all members of the United Nations 'pledge themselves to take joint and separate action in cooperation with the Organization for the achievement of the purposes set forth in Article 55'. The provisions of the Charter have the force of positive international law because the Charter is a treaty and therefore a legally binding document. All United Nations Member States must fulfil, in good faith, the obligations they have assumed under the Charter of the United Nations. This includes the obligations to promote respect for human rights, to promote observance of human rights and to cooperate with the United Nations and other nations to attain this aim. However, the Charter does not specify human rights and does not establish any specific mechanism to ensure their implementation by Member States.

6. Does international scrutiny of a country's human rights record constitute interference in the internal affairs of States?

The State is the guarantor and protector of human rights and, according to a customary rule regulating the relations between States, governments in principle have no right to intervene in the internal affairs of another State.

Some States remain sensitive and defensive regarding the scrutiny of their human rights records and continue to invoke Article 2(7) of the United Nations Charter, which stipulates that the United Nations should not intervene 'in matters which are

NO THANKS, I HAVE EVERYTHING I NEED!

essentially within the domestic jurisdiction of any State'. However, such behaviour is increasingly recognized as an attempt to avoid fulfilling certain obligations under international law and has not prevented human rights issues from being raised within the United Nations system. Moreover, the United Nations Charter recognizes that peace and stability among nations is related to the recognition of and respect for human rights, and seeks to establish conditions under which both peace and human rights, including the social and economic advancement of all peoples, can be achieved.

The United Nations Security Council unanimously declared in 1992 that the international community 'no longer can allow advancement of fundamental rights to stop at national borders'. In 1993, the Vienna Declaration and Programme of Action, adopted by the World Conference on Human Rights, stated that 'the promotion and protection of all human rights is a legitimate concern of the international community' (Article 4). Likewise, in Resolution 48/125 of 20 December 1993, the United Nations General Assembly reaffirmed that it is 'a purpose of the United Nations and the task of all Member States ...to promote and encourage respect for human rights and fundamental freedoms and to remain vigilant with regard to violations of human rights wherever they occur'. It also underlined that 'the promotion, protection and full realization of all human rights and fundamental freedoms, as legitimate concerns of the world community, should be guided by the principles of non-selectivity, impartiality and objectivity'.

The Final Outcome Document of the World Summit of 2005 underlined the responsibilities of all States to respect human rights and fundamental freedoms for all and recognized human rights as core values and principles of the United Nations.[5]

The International Bill of Human Rights

7. Which instruments constitute the International Bill of Human Rights?

The Commission on Human Rights, established in 1945 (and replaced by the Human Rights Council in 2006), was entrusted with the task of drawing up an International Bill of Human Rights, defining the human rights and freedoms referred to in the Charter. A major step in drafting the International Bill of Human Rights was realized on 10 December 1948, when the General Assembly adopted[6] the Universal Declaration of Human Rights 'as a common standard of achievement for all peoples and nations'.

The Universal Declaration of Human Rights constituted the first part of the International Bill of Human Rights. The other parts, designed to elaborate the content of the provisions of the Declaration, took many years to complete. On 16 December 1966, the United Nations General Assembly adopted two Covenants: the International Covenant on Economic, Social and Cultural Rights (ICESCR) and the International Covenant on Civil and Political Rights (ICCPR), as well as an Optional Protocol to the ICCPR, allowing for complaints to be made by individuals on violations of their rights embodied in the Covenant. In adopting these instruments, the international community not only agreed on the content of the rights set forth within the Universal Declaration, but also on measures for their implementation. A further elaboration took place when, in December 1989, the Second Optional Protocol to the ICCPR, aimed at abolishing the death penalty, was adopted by the General Assembly. The Optional Protocol to the ICESCR, adopted in December 2008, makes it possible for individuals to submit complaints on violations of the rights enshrined in the ICESCR to the Committee on Economic, Social and Cultural Rights.[7]

The adoption of these two Covenants endorsed the General Assembly resolution of 1950 that 'the enjoyment of civil and political rights and economic, social and cultural rights are interconnected and interdependent'.

8. Are all human rights equally important?

Human rights comprise civil, political, economic, social and cultural rights. The Universal Declaration of Human Rights does not distinguish the rights codified therein on the basis of their importance and does not provide for a hierarchical classification of rights. In practice, however, for several decades, economic, social and cultural rights, as opposed to civil and political rights, were viewed primarily as aspirations with few legal obligations for States. This dichotomy, fuelled to a large extent by political and ideological divisions of the Cold War, was exemplified in the elaboration and wording of two separate International Covenants, adopted in 1966, on civil and political rights and on economic, social and cultural rights. Meanwhile, in 1968 the Proclamation of Teheran by the International Conference on Human Rights confirmed that human rights and fundamental freedoms are indivisible. The overwhelming political changes following the end of the Cold War opened the door for the promotion and protection of all human rights globally, on the same footing and with the same emphasis. In 1993, the Vienna Declaration and Programme of Action adopted by the World Conference on Human Rights, recalling the Universal Declaration, reaffirmed the principle of indivisibility, interdependence and interrelatedness of all human rights. Pursuant to this principle all human rights are interconnected and equally important for the full development of the human personality and for a person's well-being. Thus, there can be no genuine and effective implementation of civil and political rights in the absence of respect for economic, social and cultural rights. The Final Outcome Document of the 2005 World Summit reaffirmed the indivisibility, interrelatedness and mutual reinforcement of all human rights, underlining that all human rights 'must be treated in a fair and equal manner, on the same footing and with the same emphasis'[8].

9. Which human rights are proclaimed in the Universal Declaration of Human Rights?

Human rights can be broadly divided into two groups. The first refers to civil and political rights, which include: the right to life, liberty, and security of person; freedom from slavery and torture; equality before the law; protection against arbitrary arrest, detention or exile; the right to a fair trial; the right to own property; political participation; the right to marriage; the fundamental freedoms of thought, conscience and religion, opinion and expression; freedom of peaceful assembly and association; and the right to take part in the government of his/her country, directly or through freely chosen representatives. The second group refers to economic, social and cultural rights, which, *inter alia*, relate to: the right to work; the right to equal pay for equal work; the right to form and join trade unions; the right to an adequate standard of living; the right to education; and the right to participate freely in cultural life.

The first Article of the Declaration expresses the universality of rights, based on the principle that all human beings are born free

and equal in dignity and rights. The second Article expresses the entitlement of all persons to the rights set out without discrimination of any kind. The fundamental principle underlying the rights proclaimed in the Declaration is contained in the Preamble to the Declaration, which recognizes the 'inherent dignity, and the equal and inalienable rights of all members of the human family'. The second part of this publication describes what is meant by each of the articles of the Universal Declaration.

10. Are States that were not members of the United Nations when the Universal Declaration of Human Rights was signed, legally bound to respect it?

Although the Universal Declaration of Human Rights is not legally binding as a treaty, over the years its main principles have acquired the status of customary international law, which States are legally bound to respect. When the Declaration was adopted, there were only fifty-eight Member States of the United Nations. Since that time, this number has more than tripled.[9] The continuing impact of the Declaration and the use made of it bears out its universal acceptance, and it has become a common reference in human rights for all nations.

The Universal Declaration, together with the Charter, served both as an inspiration and reference for the millions of people under colonial rule to achieve self-determination in the 1950s and 1960s, and many incorporated the provisions of the Declaration in their constitutions. With the global trend towards democratization, the dissolution of the Soviet Union and the disintegration of the former Yugoslavia in the 1990s, new States have emerged which have reaffirmed the principles of the Declaration in their new Constitutions.

In 1968, the international community reached a consensus at the International Conference on Human Rights in Tehran that the Universal Declaration 'states a common understanding of the peoples of the world concerning the inalienable and inviolable rights of all members of the human family and constitutes an obligation for the members of the international community'.[10] Twenty-five years later, at the World Conference on Human Rights (Vienna, Austria, 14–25 June 1993), 171 States reaffirmed that the Universal Declaration 'constitutes a common standard of achievement for all peoples and all nations'[11] and that 'it is the duty of States, regardless of their political, economic and cultural systems, to promote and protect all human rights and fundamental freedoms.'[12]

The United Nations Millennium Declaration adopted by the General Assembly on 8 September 2000 (see Question 113), under Article V on human rights, democracy and governance, calls on States 'to respect and fully uphold the Universal Declaration of Human Rights'.[13]

11. How do the International Covenants on Civil and Political Rights and on Economic, Social and Cultural Rights differ from the Universal Declaration?

The Covenants, unlike the Universal Declaration, are legally binding treaties for those States that are parties to them. Such States are thus obliged to respect the procedures for their implementation, including the submission of periodic reports on their compliance with their obligations under the Covenants. Both Covenants entered into force in 1976. Since that time 160 States have become parties to the ICESCR and 164 to the ICCPR.[14] The First Optional Protocol to the ICCPR entered into force in 1976. So far, it has been ratified by more than 111 States.[15] The Second Optional Protocol, which entered into force in 1991, has been ratified by 71 States.[16] The Optional Protocol to the ICESCR, adopted on December 2008, is not yet in force.[17]

12. What rights are protected by the International Covenant on Civil and Political Rights (ICCPR)?

This Covenant elaborates the political and civil rights identified in the Universal Declaration, which include the rights to life, privacy, fair trial, peaceful assembly, equality before the law, freedom of expression, freedom of thought, conscience and religion, and freedom from torture, as well as the prohibition of slavery in all its forms, and the rights of persons belonging to ethnic, religious and linguistic minorities. According to Article 2 of the Covenant, these rights should be immediately guaranteed by States and they should take the necessary steps in the fields of legislation and social policy to ensure this.

13. May States derogate from their obligations under the ICCPR?

Some of the rights can be suspended in times of 'public emergency which threatens the life of the nation', provided that the derogation will not involve discrimination on grounds of race, colour, sex, language, religion or social origin.

The Human Rights Committee (see Questions 14–17) in its General Comment No. 29 emphasizes two conditions that must be met prior to such derogation: (1) the situation must amount to a public emergency that threatens the life of the nation and (2) a state of emergency must be officially proclaimed by the State in question. It further states that such measures should be limited to the extent required by the situation in terms of duration, geographical coverage and material scope. If a country wants to 'opt out' in this way, it must immediately inform the Secretary-General of the United Nations. States of emergency, thus declared, unfortunately often create the conditions under which gross violations of human rights occur. In no circumstances, whether in times of peace or war, is derogation permitted under the Covenant from the following fundamental rights: the right to life, the right to equal protection before the law, freedom from torture and slavery, and freedom of thought, conscience and religion, as well as the right not to be imprisoned solely for the inability to fulfil a contractual obligation, or to be held guilty for committing a crime that did not constitute a criminal offence at the time it was committed.

14. What mechanisms are provided to monitor the implementation of the ICCPR?

Article 28 of the Covenant on Civil and Political Rights provides for the establishment of a Human Rights Committee consisting of eighteen independent experts, nominated and elected by States Parties to the Covenant, who serve in their personal capacities, which means that they are not acting on behalf of their State. The Human Rights Committee, which holds three regular sessions per year, monitors the implementation of the Covenant in a number of ways. The Committee examines periodic reports from States Parties to the Covenant on their compliance (Article 40). Such a report must be submitted by each State within one year of becoming party to the Covenant, and thereafter whenever the Committee so determines. The reports are examined in public and in the presence of the representatives of the State concerned, who may be invited to provide additional information. After examining each State report, the Committee, in closed sessions, adopts concluding observations, which reflect the main points of discussion, as well as suggestions and recommendations to the government concerned on ways in which the Covenant could be better implemented.

The Committee has progressively introduced new procedures towards more effective examination of State reports and follow-up measures. Since 2001, following the examination of a State report, the Committee may identify specific concerns as priorities and request a response from the State in question within a year. In the event of non-reporting by States (i.e. failure to submit reports), the Committee may examine a report based on information obtained from other sources.

Committee members from the same country as that of the State report being examined do not participate in its examination or in the adoption of the concluding observations. NGOs can participate actively in the meetings of the Working Groups of the Committee, held before each session, to prepare lists of questions guiding the examination of State reports. It is also the practice of NGOs to submit comments and additional information on State reports, prior to their consideration by the Committee.

The Human Rights Committee also interprets the content and meaning of specific articles of the Covenant in its 'General

Comments'. These guide the States Parties in their adherence to their obligations under the Covenant and in the preparation of State reports. The Committee can consider complaints of one State against another, provided that both have made a special declaration recognizing this role of the Committee under Article 41. To date, no such complaints have been received.

The Committee reports annually on its work to the United Nations General Assembly through the Economic and Social Council (ECOSOC).

15. How effective is the reporting procedure under the ICCPR?

Since the Human Rights Committee has no recourse beyond its comments, its power is limited and the protection of human rights depends ultimately upon compliance at the national level. However, there is a persuasive value derived from the examination of reports in public, as governments are generally sensitive to public exposure of their human rights performance. Moreover, the principal objective of the Committee is to develop a constructive dialogue with reporting States and, thereby, promote the compliance of States with the provisions of the Covenant.

Many States respond positively to the Committee's concluding observations and recommendations. Thus, Switzerland repealed a Federal Decree on political speeches that restricted the freedom of expression of foreigners without a permanent resident permit. The government of New Zealand amended laws relating to indigenous land and rights to resources, and provided public funds towards this purpose, thereby advancing the protection and promotion of the rights of the Maori, under the Covenant. The United Kingdom has taken various steps in all dependent territories to combat any discrimination on the basis of sex or race, as well as measures to eliminate differences between the rights of children born in wedlock and those born out of wedlock. New legislative amendments introduced by Sweden ensure access to pre-school, primary and secondary education, and health care to children requesting asylum, on the same conditions as children residing in Sweden. In

2008, Tunisia introduced amendments and new legislation regarding detention.

Reporting States are urged to make the text of the Covenant known, to translate it into the main local language, and to bring it to the attention of administrative and judicial authorities.

16. Can the Human Rights Committee deal with complaints from individuals?

Under the provisions of the First Optional Protocol to the ICCPR, the Committee can receive complaints known as 'communications' from individuals alleging violations of their rights under the Covenant, provided that the State concerned has ratified this Optional Protocol. Complaints are made by submitting written communications to the Committee. Representation may also be made by another person on behalf of a victim when the victim is not able to appeal to the Committee.

The Committee examines a case on its 'admissibility' and then on its 'merits' or substance in closed sessions, which means in the presence of the members of the Committee only. To be admissible, the complaint should not be anonymous; should not be an abuse of the procedure; should not be under consideration by any other international procedure; and the complainant must have exhausted all possible domestic remedies.

After confidential consideration of the communication, the Committee is empowered to bring any individual complaint that it finds admissible to the attention of the State Party concerned. The State, on its part, undertakes to provide the Committee, within six months, with a written explanation on the matter and the remedy, if any, that it may have undertaken. The Committee takes into account all written information made available to it by the initial author of the communication, by the alleged victim and by the State concerned. The Committee adopts 'views' on the merits of the case, which are forwarded to the State Party and the individual concerned, in the expectation that the State will act upon them. The Committee also makes public its decisions and views.

17. To what extent do States comply with the 'views' of the Human Rights Committee?

The Human Rights Committee expresses its 'views' in the form of legal decisions, but there is no legal enforcement mechanism. Thus the responsibility for compliance rests with the State concerned. States comply for various reasons, including a genuine wish to fulfil the obligations of the Covenant and a desire to enhance their international image.

When compliance does occur, it is not always in full and can be reluctant. In a case against the Netherlands, the Committee found a violation with which the Netherlands did not agree, but 'out of respect for the Committee' made an *ex gratia* payment to the complainant.

There are many examples, however, of States Parties complying fully with the 'views' of the Committee. Finland revised its Aliens Act in order to make the provisions governing the detention of aliens compatible with the Covenant, in compliance with the Committee's 'views'. It also paid compensation to the victim. Likewise, Mauritius changed its law in response to the Committee's 'views' upholding the complaints of a number of Mauritian women who claimed that the Government had arbitrarily interfered with family life and discriminated on the grounds of sex. Latvia changed legislation that discriminated against its Russian minority, in order to provide members of the minority with the possibility of gaining access to public office. Other positive responses, relating to the Committee's 'views' on communications under the Optional Protocol, have been forthcoming from a number of countries including Canada, Colombia, Ecuador, Peru, and Trinidad and Tobago.

To promote compliance with its 'views', the Committee designates a Special Rapporteur with the mandate to request written information from States Parties on any measures taken in pursuance of the Committee's 'views'.

The Committee has recently issued (November 2008) General Comment No. 33, analysing and clarifying the communication procedure and the obligations of States Parties under the Optional Protocol to ICCPR.[18]

18. Which rights are protected by the International Covenant on Economic, Social and Cultural Rights (ICESCR)?

The rights guaranteed in the Covenant include the rights to: work; favourable conditions of work and equal pay for equal work; form and join trade unions; social security; an adequate standard of living, including adequate food, clothing and housing; protection of the family; the highest attainable standard of physical and mental health; education; participate in cultural life; benefit from scientific progress; and protection of an author's moral and material interests resulting from scientific, literary or artistic production. According to Article 2 of the Covenant, each State Party to the Covenant agrees to 'take steps... to the maximum of its available resources, with a view to achieving progressively the full realization of the rights recognized' in the Covenant.

19. What mechanisms are there for the implementation of the ICESCR?

The body that monitors the implementation of the Covenant is the Committee on Economic, Social and Cultural Rights (CESCR), which was established by ECOSOC in 1985. It is composed of eighteen independent experts, nominated and elected by ECOSOC, who serve in their personal capacity. The Committee reports annually to ECOSOC regarding its consideration of State reports and other activities.

The supervisory mechanism currently provided for under the Covenant is the periodic State reporting procedure. The Committee publicly examines periodic reports submitted by States Parties, which reflect the measures adopted, the progress made and the problems and challenges encountered in meeting their obligations under the Covenant. Representatives from States Parties are entitled to be present when the Committee examines the report and are engaged in a constructive dialogue. They may be asked to furnish additional information. The Committee also takes account of relevant information from United Nations specialized agencies relating to their particular area of expertise, and invites submissions of written and oral statements by non-governmental organizations. The Committee may request that the State Party accept a mission comprising a visit to the country of several of its members to assess the situation and subsequent need for technical and advisory services.

After a constructive dialogue with a State Party regarding its report, the Committee adopts its concluding observations. These reflect the main points of discussion and identify positive aspects as well as principal subjects of concern. Factors and difficulties impeding the implementation of the Covenant are also identified and suggestions and recommendations are put forward. These observations are an important source of public information.

After several years of consideration, the Optional Protocol to the ICESCR was adopted on 10 December 2008. The Protocol provides a complaints mechanism similar to the one offered by the Optional Protocol to the ICCPR. According to the Protocol, individual complaints, called 'communications', can be submitted by or on behalf of individuals or groups claiming to be victims of a violation of any of the economic, social or cultural rights enshrined in the ICESCR.

20. What specific measures has the Committee on Economic, Social and Cultural Rights (CESCR) developed in dealing with State reports?

The Committee has revised the reporting procedure in a number of ways to assist States Parties in the implementation of the Covenant. When additional information supplied by the State Party does not meet the requirements of the Committee, and the situation is of immediate and grave concern, the Committee may request the States concerned to allow an information-gathering mission. Their subsequent report remains confidential but the Committee will adopt a set of observations based on the results of the missions.

To encourage States to submit their reports on time, the Committee has adopted the practice of scheduling meetings to consider the situation of Covenant rights in particular countries, even in the absence of a State Party report. The Committee, in this case, relies on information from a range of sources, such as international and regional organizations, and NGOs. The latter may also, at any point, submit written information concerning the enjoyment of rights within States Parties to the Covenant. This has enabled the Committee to initiate requests to States for a response to *ad hoc* reports from alternative sources regarding situations of immediate and grave concern.

In January 2009, the Committee issued new Guidelines for the States Parties to the Covenant on how to submit their reports. These Guidelines follow the harmonized guidelines on reporting under the international human rights treaties. Under the new procedure, the States should submit a core document which will provide general information about the human rights situation in the State and another document on the situation of the rights enshrined in the Covenant.

21. How does the CESCR assist States Parties in implementing the ICESCR?

During each of its sessions, the Committee holds a day of general discussion regarding a specific right or a particular aspect of the Covenant. Some of the focal issues have been: the right to food, health, and education; the role of social and economic indicators; the rights of older people and the ageing; the right to take part in cultural life; and the impact of globalization on the enjoyment of economic, social and cultural rights. These discussions are often a preparatory phase for the drafting of a General Comment, and are summarized in the Committee's annual report to ECOSOC. The Committee provides normative interpretations of the Covenant rights and issues related thereto by means of 'General Comments'. The purpose of these is to assist States Parties in fulfilling their reporting obligations and to assist and promote progressively the full realization of the rights recognized in the Covenant. In its General Comment No. 3, for example, the Committee clarified two provisions in the Covenant on which States Parties must take immediate action. These are the non-discrimination provisions and the obligation to 'take steps' that are 'deliberate, concrete and targeted as clearly as possible towards meeting the obligations recognized in the Covenant'. The Committee also notes in this General Comment that it is the obligation of all States Parties 'to ensure the satisfaction of, at the very least, minimum essential levels of each of the rights' in the Covenant. The only exception is if a State can show that resource constraints make it impossible to act.

Other 'General Comments' focused on such issues as the right to adequate housing, the right to (primary) education, the right to adequate food, the right to the highest attainable standard of health, the right of everyone to benefit from the protection of the moral and material interests resulting from any scientific, literary or artistic production of which he/she is the author, the right to work and the right to social security, as well as the right to water.

22. How has the CESCR elaborated on the nature of States' obligations under the ICESCR?

In various General Comments, the Committee has elaborated the notion of States Parties' obligations. The Committee uses a typology of these obligations to respect, protect and fulfil the provisions within the Covenant.

Obligations to respect are obligations calling on States to refrain from actions that may contravene a provision in the Covenant. For example, General Comment 14 requires States to respect the right to health by providing equal access to health services, by not impeding individual or group access and by refraining from any actions that impede people's health (e.g. high levels of pollution). Under the right to housing in General Comment No. 7, the Committee requires States Parties to respect this right by refraining from forced evictions under any circumstances.

Obligations to protect are obligations on States to protect individuals against acts by third parties that violate their human rights. For the right to health, the obligation to protect requires States to take the necessary legislative and other measures to ensure non-discrimination and equal access where services are provided by the private sector. States must also ensure that private parties do not harm the health of others. According to General Comment No. 4 on the right to housing, States Parties should protect individuals from abuse by non-state actors. When infringements do occur, States must act to ensure that no deprivation occurs. They must therefore implement effective measures to protect from, *inter alia*, evictions, harassment, discrimination, and withdrawal of services.

Obligations to fulfil are obligations that require States to provide or facilitate a particular service contributing to the implementation of a certain right. In respect of the right to health, States must: adopt a national health policy and allocate sufficient funds to it; provide or create the conditions whereby people can have adequate access to health services; and promote measures ensuring the preconditions for health. With regard to the right to housing, States fulfil their obligations by taking housing into account in government regulation, expenditure, subsidies and other relevant areas.

Economic and other issues may preclude the immediate realization of some of the rights under the ICESCR, and the Covenant therefore recognizes the notion of their progressive realization. The Covenant enumerates various means to be undertaken by States Parties 'with a view to achieving, progressively, the full realization of the rights recognized' in the Covenant (Article 2(1)). In its General Comment No. 3, the Committee stated that the 'minimum core obligation to ensure the satisfaction of, at the very least, minimum essential levels of each of the rights is incumbent upon every State party.' In subsequent General Comments, the Committee has identified core obligations, which are aimed at the realization of the most basic elements of each right, without which that right would lose its rationale and its meaning. For example, under the right to health in General Comment 14, the Committee recognizes that the right will be progressively realized, but sets a threshold below which States should not go. States must provide: basic health care, comprising maternal and child health care (including planning); immunization; treatment of common diseases and injuries; essential drugs; preconditions for health i.e. health education; knowledge of basic nutrition; and basic sanitation (including safe water). In addition, they must attempt to increase the food supply, if necessary.

In General Comment 13, the Committee defines specific obligations of the States Parties regarding the right to education. States should ensure availability, accessibility, acceptability and adaptability of education for all.

23. Which special procedures have been established for the protection and promotion of the rights in the ICESCR?

Special Procedures have been developed towards this end (see Question 65). Those relating specifically to economic and social rights are reflected in the appointment of the following Special Rapporteurs.

In 1998, the Commission on Human Rights appointed a Special Rapporteur on the Right to Education whose mandate included, *inter alia*: to report on the status, throughout the world, of the progressive realization of the right to education, including access to primary education and the difficulties encountered in its implementation. Moreover, the Special Rapporteur should provide, as appropriate, assistance to governments in devising and adopting urgent plans of action to secure the progressive implementation, within a reasonable timescale, of the principle of compulsory primary education, free of charge, for all. The Special Rapporteur's mandate was extended for three years by the Human Rights Council in 2008. An Independent Expert on Human Rights and Extreme Poverty was appointed by the Commission on Human Rights in 1998. The report of the independent expert to the Commission at its 58th session, in 2002, focused on concrete and workable methods to combat poverty that incorporated the voice of the poorest populations at all levels. The Commission on Human Rights, in a subsequent resolution, reiterated the link between human rights and extreme poverty, which constitutes a violation of human dignity and renders democracy fragile and popular participation difficult. The Expert's mandate was extended by the Human Rights Council in 2008, for three years.

In 2000, the Commission appointed a Special Rapporteur on the Right to Food. The Rapporteur's second report to the Commission (2002) examined the justiciability of the right with a particular focus on the rules governing humanitarian assistance. The report also dealt with the issue of international trade and human rights, including the implications of the new round of trade negotiations agreed at the fourth World Trade Organization (WTO) Ministerial Conference held in Doha, in November 2001. In the conclusion, the Rapporteur noted that 815 million people are still suffering from hunger and malnutrition while 36 million die each year from hunger-related illnesses. In the recommendations, it was stressed that the justiciability of the right to food be recognized, furthered and established; the importance of the observance of the principles of neutrality, impartiality and humanitarian motives in distributing humanitarian assistance be acknowledged; and that negotiations on trade issues should not conflict with human rights. In 2007, the Rapporteur's mandate was extended, by the Human Rights Council, for three years.

In 2000, the Commission also appointed a Special Rapporteur on Adequate Housing as a component of the right to an adequate standard of living (as reflected in the Universal Declaration of

Human Rights, Article 25, and various other international treaties). In the report to the 58th Session of the Commission on Human Rights (2002), the Rapporteur included themes of discrimination and segregation in the context of the World Conference against Racism and the impact of globalization. The Rapporteur reviewed the relevant dimension of the Durban Declaration and Programme of Action and emphasized the need to place the issues related to discrimination in housing firmly within a human rights framework. These issues relate not only to race, class and gender, but also to poverty and economic marginalization. The Human Rights Council extended the mandate of the Rapporteur in 2007, for three years.

In 2002, the Commission appointed a Special Rapporteur on the Right of Everyone to the Enjoyment of the Highest Attainable Standard of Physical and Mental Health whose mandate includes collaboration with, *inter alia*, the Joint United Nations Programme on HIV/AIDS (UNAIDS). In 2007, the Human Rights Council extended the mandate of the Rapporteur for three years.

PLANTU

In 2008, the Human Rights Council appointed an Independent Expert on the Issue of Human Rights Obligations Related to Access to Safe Drinking Water and Sanitation. The Expert should identify, promote and exchange best practices on the subject. She is also entitled to further clarify the content of human rights obligations in relation to access to safe drinking water and sanitation.

In March 2009, the Human Rights Council established the mandate of the Independent Expert on the promotion and protection of cultural rights, in an effort to enhance this 'neglected' group of rights.

24. What other United Nations human rights instruments are there besides the International Bill of Human Rights?

There are many conventions, declarations and recommendations adopted by the General Assembly and other bodies of the United Nations that elaborate in more detail the rights set out in the Universal Declaration and the International Covenants, and that also include certain rights not specified in the International Bill of Human Rights. The declarations and recommendations apply to all Member States of the United Nations but do not have the same legal force as the conventions, which are legally binding upon States that have become parties to them.

States are encouraged to observe international standards, to ratify or accede to international human rights treaties and to incorporate them in their national legislation.

Among the international instruments are those relating to: the right to life; the prevention of discrimination and the rights of persons belonging to minorities; the rights of indigenous peoples and refugees; and the protection of human rights in times of war (see Question 69). All of these instruments are discussed below. Other relevant standards include: the Convention against Torture and Other Cruel, Inhuman or Degrading Treatment or Punishment (see Questions 26–29 and Part II, Article 5); the Convention on the Rights of the Child (see Questions 42–45); the Convention relating to the Status of Refugees and the related Protocol (see Questions

54–57); the Convention on the Elimination of All Forms of Racial Discrimination (see Questions 31–35); the Convention on the Elimination of All Forms of Discrimination Against Women (see Questions 36–41); the Convention on the Rights of Persons with Disabilities (see Question 53) and the International Convention for the Protection of All Persons from Enforced Disappearance (see Question 30).

International instruments concerning specific human rights issues

25. What instruments are there to prevent and punish the crime of genocide?

In December 1948, the United Nations General Assembly adopted the Convention on the Prevention and Punishment of the Crime of Genocide. It came into force in 1951 and by the end of May 2009 had been ratified by 140 States.[19] Genocide, in the terms of Article 2 of the Convention, means 'any of the following acts committed with intent to destroy, in whole or in part, a national, ethnical, racial or religious group, as such: (a) Killing members of the group; (b) Causing serious bodily or mental harm to members of the group; (c) Deliberately inflicting on the group conditions of life calculated to bring about its physical destruction in whole or in part; (d) Imposing measures intended to prevent births within the group; (e) Forcibly transferring children of the group to another group.' Genocide is designated as a crime under international law, whether committed in time of war or of peace, and is defined as a crime against humanity.

Provision is made in Article 6 of the Convention for persons charged with committing genocide to be tried either by a competent tribunal in the State where the act was committed or by an international penal tribunal that has been accepted as competent by States

Parties to the Convention. Moreover, it is generally recognized that any State has jurisdiction over the crime of genocide.

The crime of genocide is also included in the Statutes of all international criminal courts: the International Criminal Court (see Question 71); the International Criminal Tribunal for Rwanda; the International Criminal Tribunal for former Yugoslavia (see Question 70); and the Special Court for Sierra Leone (see Question 70).

26. What instruments and procedures have been developed to prevent and punish torture?

The Convention against Torture and Other Cruel, Inhuman or Degrading Treatment or Punishment, adopted by the United Nations General Assembly in December 1984, came into force on 26 June 1987. As of 31 May 2009, 146 States had ratified the Convention.[20]

The Convention calls upon States Parties to take effective legislative, administrative, judicial and other measures to prevent torture and to make it a punishable offence. The Convention defines torture as 'any act by which severe pain or suffering, whether physical or mental, is intentionally inflicted on a person for such purposes as obtaining from him or a third person information or a confession, punishing him for an act he or a third person has committed or is suspected of having committed, or intimidating or coercing him or a third person, or for any reason based on dis-crimination of any kind, when such pain or suffering is inflicted by or at the instigation of or with the consent or acquiescence of a public official or other person acting in an official capacity. It does not include pain or suffering arising only from, inherent in, or incidental to lawful sanctions' (Article 1).

The Convention allows no derogation from the prohibition of torture. No exceptional circumstances, whether a state of war or a threat of war, internal political instability or any other public emergency, may be invoked to justify torture (Article 2). Moreover, pursuant to Article 5, each State Party has the obligation to estab-lish its jurisdiction over such offences in cases where the alleged offender is present in any territory under its jurisdiction and it does not extradite him to another State. States Parties must ensure legal provisions with a view to ensuring for victims of torture an enforceable right to fair and adequate compensation, including the means for rehabilitation and redress (see also Part II, Article 5).

27. Which mechanism ensures the implementation of the Convention against Torture?

The Convention provides for the establishment of a Committee against Torture, consisting of ten experts who serve in their personal capacity. The members of the Committee are elected by the States Parties by secret ballot from a list of persons nominated by the States.

The Committee has the competence to monitor the implementation of the Convention in the following ways: it examines reports from States Parties on the measures they have taken to give effect to the Convention; and it receives and considers communications from individuals (or on behalf of individuals) who claim to be victims of a violation of a right guaranteed by the Convention as well as inter-State complaints, provided that the State or States concerned have made declarations recognizing the competence of the Committee to receive and consider such communications. As of 31 May 2009, 67 States have made a declaration recognizing that competence of the Committee.[21]

The Committee has the power to initiate confidential inquiries, in cooperation with the State Party concerned, into alleged situations of systematic torture. The findings of the Committee are transmitted to the State Party under examination, and a summary account of the inquiry may, after consultation with the State Party, be included in the Committee's annual report to the United Nations General Assembly.

The Protocol to the Convention against Torture, adopted in 2002 and which entered into force on 22 June 2006, establishes an international monitoring mechanism for the effective implementation of the Convention. The Protocol provides for the creation of an international body of experts (the Subcommittee on Prevention of Torture) which can make visits to places of detention and monitor the application of the Convention by the States Parties. It also provides for the establishment of national mechanisms by the States in order to prevent torture in their territory. As of 31 May 2009, 47 States have ratified the Protocol.[22]

28. Which other United Nations procedures have been established to prevent torture?

The Special Rapporteur on Torture, initially appointed by the Commission on Human Rights in 1985 (the mandate was renewed by the Human Rights Council in 2008 for three years) has an obligation to examine questions relevant to torture worldwide. The Special Rapporteur may seek and receive credible and reliable information and is expected to respond without delay. An urgent action procedure allows for prompt action in circumstances where there is an identifiable risk of torture. In circumstances where information suggests that torture is occurring on a persistent basis, the Rapporteur may undertake a fact-finding mission to a particular country. This is, however, dependent upon an invitation from the country concerned.

Any individual, group, NGO, intergovernmental organization or government that has knowledge of the occurrence of acts of torture or other forms of ill-treatment can bring the information to the Special Rapporteur's attention, without the exhaustion of domestic remedies and without having to comply with any specific formality in doing so. A comprehensive report is submitted to the Human Rights Council (before 2006 to the Commission on Human Rights) annually, and, since 1999, annual interim reports to the General Assembly are also submitted. The Special Rapporteur's 1993 report to the Commission on Human Rights concluded that the elimination of torture is a matter of political will and its persistence is testimony to the failure of political will. The Special Rapporteur in the 2002 report to the Commission on Human Rights recommended that the highest authorities should publicly condemn torture. Furthermore, it was recommended that secret places of detention should be abolished by law and that interrogation should only take place at official centres, that incommunicado detention should be prohibited by law and that training courses and manuals should be provided for police and security personnel.

In his 2008 report to the Human Rights Council, the Special Rapporteur underlined the importance of considering a gender sensitive definition of torture and of seeing the torture protection framework in connection with a wide range of human rights guarantees.

29. Are there any regional instruments for the prevention of torture?

The European Convention for the Prevention of Torture and Inhuman or Degrading Treatment or Punishment (1987) entered into force on 1 February 1989.[23] The Convention established the Committee for the Prevention of Torture (CPT), which is made up of independent experts. States Parties must allow members of the Committee unrestricted access and complete freedom of movement in places of detention on their territory. The experts report on their findings regarding the implementation of the Convention. Information from non-governmental organizations provides important additional material for the Committee. The reports are sent to the governments concerned and remain confidential unless the government in question fails to take remedial action, in which case the Committee can make its concern public. Two new protocols to the Convention came into force on 3 March 2002. The first opens the Convention to non-member States of the Council of Europe (with the approval of the Committee of Ministers) and the second introduces technical changes, including the renewal of CPT membership every two years.

The Inter-American Convention to Prevent and Punish Torture, adopted in 1985 by the Organization of American States, entered into force in 1987.[24] Under this Convention, the Inter-American Commission on Human Rights is entitled to analyse the situation concerning the prevention and elimination of torture in the region and to report annually on this (see Question 100).

30. What instruments are there to protect persons from enforced disappearances?

Enforced or involuntary disappearances constitute grave human rights violations. All around the world, persons are arrested, detained or abducted, without being able to identify their whereabouts or enjoy their rights. The United Nations have been active on this subject since 1980, in an effort to prevent enforced disappearances.

In February 1980, the Commission on Human Rights decided to establish a Working Group, consisting of five members of the Commission, to examine questions relevant to enforced or involuntary disappearances. With the adoption by the General Assembly of the Declaration on the Protection of all Persons from Enforced Disappearances, in 1992, the Working Group was also entrusted with monitoring the progress made by States in applying the provisions of the Declaration and to provide assistance in its implementation. The mandate of the Working Group was renewed by the Human Rights Council, in 2008, for a period of three years.

The question of impunity for acts of enforced or involuntary disappearances constitutes an important part of the Working Group's work, since it is also a part of its mandate. The Working Group has issued several General Comments in order to clarify the meaning of the articles of the Declaration, including the General Comment on the definition of enforced or involuntary disappearances.

The Rome Statute of the International Criminal Court defines acts of enforced disappearance as crimes against humanity. In 2006 the United Nations General Assembly adopted the Convention for the Protection of All Persons from Enforced Disappearance. It affirms that enforced disappearances constitute a crime against humanity when practised in a widespread or systematic manner. It also creates an obligation for States to make the offence of enforced disappearance punishable by appropriate penalties and establishes the right of the victims for reparation. As at 31 May 2009, the Convention had not yet entered into force.[25] The Convention envisages the establishment of a Committee on Enforced Disappearances which will examine the States Parties' reports. Articles 31 and 32 of the Convention provide the possibility for the Committee to receive and consider individual complaints, provided that the State Party has made a declaration to accept this competence of the Committee.

The Inter-American Convention on the Forced Disappearance of Persons, which entered into force in 1996, is, so far, the only regional standard-setting instrument for the protection of persons from enforced disappearance.[26]

31. What instruments are there to prevent and eliminate racial discrimination?

The fundamental principle of non-discrimination is enshrined in Article 1 of the United Nations Charter (see Question 5) and is reflected in the International Bill of Human Rights and all other major human rights instruments. There are two specific instruments in this field that relate to racial discrimination and discrimination against women.

The International Convention on the Elimination of All Forms of Racial Discrimination came into force in 1969 and, as of 31 May 2009, it had been ratified by more than 170 States.[27] It represents the most comprehensive United Nations instrument regarding discrimination, which includes 'distinction, exclusion, restriction or preference' on the grounds of 'race, colour, descent, or national or ethnic origin'. States Parties to the Convention undertake to pursue a policy of eliminating racial discrimination in all its forms. Moreover, States must ensure the protection of certain racial groups and guarantee their members full and equal enjoyment of human rights and fundamental freedoms.

Another very important instrument in this field is the UNESCO Declaration on Race and Racial Prejudice, which was adopted by acclamation in 1978 by UNESCO's General Conference, together with the resolution for the implementation of this Declaration. The resolution urges Member States to report through the Director-General to the General Conference on the steps they have taken to put into effect the principles of the Declaration. International non-governmental organizations are also called upon to cooperate and assist in the implementation of the principles set out in this Declaration.

32. How is the International Convention on the Elimination of All Forms of Racial Discrimination implemented?

A Committee on the Elimination of Racial Discrimination (CERD) comprising eighteen independent experts, established under Article 8 of the Convention, supervises governmental compliance. The

NOTES

Imprimé en France. - JOUVE, 1, rue du Docteur Sauvé, 53100 MAYENNE
N° 493220S - Dépôt légal : Octobre 2009

NOTES

Committee has several functions. Its main task is the examination of periodic reports from States Parties on the measures they have taken to implement the Convention. Governments are represented at the examination of their reports, and the Committee pursues a strategy of informal dialogue to encourage governments to comply with their obligations. In its final report, the Committee makes concluding observations on each State report, suggesting and recommending ways in which the Convention could be more effectively implemented. Some States have taken account of this by amending their constitutions and domestic laws to make racial discrimination a punishable offence, as well as by establishing education programmes and new agencies to deal with problems of racial discrimination.

The Committee is also developing measures aimed at the prevention of racial discrimination. These include 'early warning' procedures aimed at preventing existing problems from escalating into overt conflict, and confidence-building initiatives towards strengthening tolerance and peaceful coexistence. It also undertakes urgent preventive action in response to acute situations arising from serious violations of the Convention. In this context, the Committee has initiated 'on the spot' visits by sending missions to areas of particular concern.[28]

The Committee adopts General Recommendations, which serve to interpret the content of the provisions of the Convention and to assist States in the implementation of their obligations. For example, its General Recommendation XXIX on Article 1, paragraph 1 of the Convention clarifies the term 'descent'. The Committee concluded that this does not solely refer to 'race' but is relevant to other prohibited grounds of discrimination, including discrimination 'based on forms of social stratification such as caste and analogous systems of inherited status', which negatively affect the equal enjoyment of human rights. The Recommendation includes comprehensive practical measures for States to adopt, as appropriate.

The Committee reports annually to the General Assembly of the United Nations and is dependent upon the Assembly to endorse and give authority to its suggestions and general recommendations. Another function of the Committee is to apply the

procedure (not yet invoked by any State) that allows it to deal with inter-State complaints.

33. Can individuals complain to the CERD about violations of the Convention?

Article 14 of the Convention allows the Committee to examine, in closed session, complaints from individuals or groups of individuals against States, provided that the State concerned has recognized the right of individual petition. This procedure became operative in December 1982. As of 31 May 2009, 50 States had recognized this right.[29] The Committee has considered a number of cases and published its opinions on them.

34. What other initiatives have been taken by the United Nations to combat racism and racial discrimination?

Between 1973 and 2003 the General Assembly proclaimed three decades to combat racism and racial discrimination. Despite the efforts of the international community, the objectives of the decades have not been attained. The deep-rooted, underlying causes and institutionalization of racism, racial discrimination and related intolerance persist in various forms in most societies. Such practices recognize no national or cultural boundaries, and often result in gross violations of human rights, ranging from discriminating practices to violent conflicts. Growing international concern prompted the General Assembly (in 1997) to convene a World Conference Against Racism, Racial Discrimination, Xenophobia and Related Intolerance (Durban, South Africa, 31 August – 8 September 2001). The conference aimed, among other things, 'to reappraise the obstacles to progress in the field and to identify ways to overcome them' and 'to formulate concrete recommendations to further action-oriented national, regional and international measures towards this end.'

The outcome of the World Conference is reflected in the Durban Declaration and Programme of Action. The Declaration

contains the fundamental principles to be considered, while the Programme of Action provides a framework of concrete measures to be taken to combat racism, racial discrimination, xenophobia and related intolerance. These measures should be taken by: States and regional organizations; development institutions; UN specialized agencies; international and national NGOs and other sectors of civil society; intergovernmental organizations; the media and Internet providers; and politicians and political parties in their respective spheres.

The UN General Assembly has proclaimed 21 March as the International Day for the Elimination of Racial Discrimination.

35. What action is being taken as a follow-up to the World Conference against Racism, Racial Discrimination, Xenophobia and Related Intolerance (2001)?

A voluntary fund has been established to support, *inter alia*, the implementation of the Durban Declaration and Programme of Action and subsequent measures to follow up their respective provisions. The Office of the United Nations High Commissioner for Human Rights (OHCHR) will spearhead the implementation of the Durban Agenda. The UN High Commissioner for Human Rights will present an annual progress report on the implementation of these provisions to the Human Rights Council and to the General Assembly in consultation with a group of five eminent independent experts, which has been set up for this purpose.

A new anti-discrimination unit has been created within the OHCHR, which, *inter alia*, will create a database of resources and 'good practices' concerning the fight against racism.

The Durban Programme of Action calls on States, in dialogue with NGOs, to develop action-oriented national policies as well as domestic and multilateral cooperation programmes to 'promote diversity, equality of opportunity, tolerance, social justice and equity' and provide information on these actions to the OHCHR.

General Recommendation XXVIII of CERD relates to the follow-up to the World Conference. The role of CERD as the

principal body to combat racism and racial discrimination is recognized in the Durban Declaration and Programme of Action. The Recommendation outlines the measures that States should take to strengthen the implementation of the Convention.

The mandate of the Special Rapporteur on contemporary forms of racism, racial discrimination, xenophobia and related intolerance was established by the Commission on Human Rights in 1993, and was renewed by the Human Rights Council in 2008 for three years.

Another initiative introduced was the creation, in 2002, by the Commission on Human Rights, of a Working Group of Experts on People of African Descent with a wide mandate aimed at elaborating proposals for the elimination of racial discrimination against people of African descent. The Working Group consists of five independent experts. Its mandate was extended in 2008 by the Human Rights Council for a period of three years. In addition, an ad hoc Committee on the elaboration of complementary standards was created in 2002 by the Commission on Human Rights. The role of the Committee is to prepare and propose complementary international standards to strengthen and update international instruments against racism.

In order to assess the progress made since 2001, the Durban Review Conference, known as Durban II, took place in Geneva on 20-24 April 2009. Its Outcome Document calls for further intensification of efforts to combat racism and stresses the need to identify concrete measures and initiatives in this field.[30]

International instruments related to the protection of specific groups

36. What instrument is there to combat discrimination against women and how is it implemented?

The Convention on the Elimination of All Forms of Discrimination against Women was adopted by the United Nations General Assembly on 18 December 1979, and entered into force on 2 September 1981. By now there are more than 185 States Parties to this Convention.[31] The aim of the Convention is to promote equality between men and women and to prevent discrimination against women. It specifies, in particular, such forms of discrimination as forced marriages, domestic violence and insufficient access to education, health care and public life, as well as discrimination at work.

These issues were identified at an early stage by the Commission on the Status of Women (a body of governmental representatives), which was established in 1946 with the mandate to further gender equality. It was also given the task of drafting the Convention. The Commission has also been concerned with practical measures to ensure the implementation of women's rights. The Commission can receive complaints (communications) relating to the status of women. On the basis of these complaints and the replies of States, the Commission makes recommendations to ECOSOC concerning actions to be taken on emerging patterns and trends of injustice and discrimination against women.

The Committee on the Elimination of Discrimination against Women (CEDAW), a body of twenty-three independent experts established under Article 17 of the Convention, monitors the implementation of the Convention. It considers periodic reports from States Parties regarding their compliance with the provisions of the Convention. The Committee also makes general recommendations on specific Articles of the Convention, or on issues related to the Convention. In 1992, General Recommendation No. 19 was made on the issue of violence against women. Though not specifically mentioned in the Convention, this issue is deemed by the

Committee as constituting discrimination against women and, as such, a violation, *inter alia*, of Articles 1 to 4 of the Convention. The recommendation suggests specific measures, which States should take to protect women from violence.

In December 2000, an Optional Protocol to the Convention came into force. The communications may be submitted to the Committee by or on behalf of any individual or group claiming to be a victim of a violation of any of the rights under the Convention.[32]

The Committee also submits an annual report to the General Assembly, containing a record of the examination of State reports, concluding observations and general recommendations.

37. What strategies are there to ensure gender equality?

Gender equality can be defined as 'an equal visibility, empowerment and participation of both sexes in all spheres of public and private life. Gender equality is the opposite of gender inequality, not of gender difference and aims to promote the full participation of women and men in society'.[33]

Strategies on gender equality are broadly aimed at integrating the human rights of women into all United Nations activities, as well as creating special mechanisms to deal with violations of those rights specifically concerning women. In order to further promote the rights of women, the United Nations convened several world conferences: in Mexico City, Mexico (1975),[34] Copenhagen, Denmark (1980)[35] and Nairobi, Kenya (1985). The latter adopted the 'Nairobi Forward-looking Strategies for the Advancement of Women to the Year 2000', which are aimed at the achievement of a genuine equality of women in all spheres of life and the elimination of all forms and manifestations of discrimination against them.

The Fourth World Conference on Women, which took place in Beijing, China, from 4 to 15 September 1995, confirmed the importance of action to ensure the advancement of women. The Beijing Declaration and Platform for Action, adopted at the Conference, called for their full incorporation into the development process, improvement of their status in society, and the provision of greater opportunities for education. Moreover, States commit-

ted themselves to including an effective gender dimension in their policies and institutions.

The Vienna Declaration and Programme of Action (adopted at the World Conference on Human Rights in 1993) also called for increased integration of women's rights into the United Nations human rights system. It furthermore endorsed the need to recognize women's rights as an integral part of human rights, as well as the special needs of women and their equal participation in all spheres of life. It also pressed for a more vigorous implementation of the Convention on the Elimination of All Forms of Discrimination against Women.

38. What progress has been made since the World Conference on Women in Beijing (1995)?

In June 2000, a special session of the UN General Assembly was held, entitled 'Beijing + 5 Women 2000: Gender Equality, Development and Peace for the 21st Century'. The main objectives of this special session were to review the implementation of the Platform of Action adopted in Beijing and to consider additional initiatives that would enhance its implementation.

Governments had been asked to report on their action to implement the Platform for Action in the twelve critical areas of concern identified in the document. The response rate of over 80 per cent was of itself indicative of the strong worldwide commitment to the goal of gender equality. Review of the national reports reflected profound changes in the status and role of women since the start of the United Nations Decade for Women in 1976. Women have entered the labour force in unprecedented numbers, increasing their ability to participate in economic decision-making at various levels, starting with the household. Women, individually and collectively, have been major actors in civil society throughout the world, stimulating increased awareness of the gender equality dimensions of all issues, and demanding a role in national and global decision-making processes.

The role of non-governmental organizations, especially women's organizations, in putting the concerns of women and gender equality on the national and international agenda was acknowledged by many governments. Despite progress in many areas, it was recognized that renewed and sustained effort was required towards the implementation of the goals set by the Platform of Action. These were reflected in the 'Outcome Document' of the Session and indicated twelve areas for action. Two areas – violence and poverty – continue to be major obstacles to gender equality worldwide. Globalization has added further dimensions to both areas, creating new challenges for the implementation of the Platform. These include the trafficking of women and girls, the changing nature of armed conflict, the growing gap between nations and the detachment of macroeconomic policy from social protection concerns. The Political Declaration and the Outcome Document strongly confirm that the Beijing Platform of Action remains the reference point for governmental commitment to women's advancement and gender equality.

39. What is meant by 'mainstreaming a gender perspective'?

The Commission on Human Rights by its Resolution 2002/50 called for 'intensified effort at the international level to integrate the equal status of women and the human rights of women into

the mainstream of United Nations system-wide activity' in order to achieve gender equality.

The idea of mainstreaming a gender perspective calls for assessing the implications for women and men of any proposed action concerning policy, programmes, or legislation. The objective is to ensure that the experiences and concerns of both genders interact with and are reflected in every aspect of policy and programme development and implementation, in all political, economic and societal spheres, thereby fostering equality between men and women. The Resolution describes in detail how this is to be achieved. A good example of the interpretation of gender mainstreaming within legally binding instruments is the inclusion of a gender perspective throughout the 1998 Rome Statute of the International Criminal Court.

The Commission on the Status of Women, established by the ECOSOC in 1946, has, since 1995, included among its tasks the regular review of the critical areas of concern defined by the Beijing Platform for Action. Since 1996, the ECOSOC has entrusted the Commission with the task of mainstreaming a gender perspective in the United Nations' activities.

Of particular interest is the Resolution on 'Women and Peace and Security' adopted by Security Council Resolution 1325 (2000), which, *inter alia*, calls for a gender perspective to be adopted when negotiating and implementing peace agreements.

In May 2007, in response to the ECOSOC Resolutions 9 and 36 of 2006, the Secretary-General of the United Nations submitted a report on the subject of mainstreaming a gender perspective throughout all spheres of the United Nations' activities.

40. What international standards and other measures have been adopted to combat violence against women?

The Rome Statute of the International Criminal Court specifically defines rape, sexual slavery, enforced prostitution, forced pregnancy, enforced sterilization and any other form of sexual violence of comparable gravity, both as crimes against humanity and as war crimes (see Question 71).

The Committee on the Elimination of Discrimination Against Women, in its General Recommendation No. 19 (29 January 1992) entitled 'Violence against Women', states that 'gender-based violence' is a form of discrimination that seriously inhibits women's ability to enjoy rights and freedoms on a basis of equality with men. The Recommendation also specifies the type of action a State should take to eliminate violence within the home.

The Recommendation states that such violence impairs or nullifies the enjoyment of many fundamental human rights by women, including: the right to life; the right not to be subject to torture or cruelty, inhuman or degrading treatment or punishment; the right to equal protection according to humanitarian norms in time of international or internal armed conflict; the right to liberty and security of person; the right to equal protection under the law; the right to equality in the family; the right to the highest standard attainable of physical and mental health; and the right to just and favourable conditions of work. In so doing, the recommendation sets out a comprehensive account of what constitutes gender-related violence and is therefore prohibited.

The Declaration on the Elimination of Violence against Women, adopted by the General Assembly in 1993,[36] calls on all States to take measures to prevent and punish violence against women. The UN General Assembly adopted a number of resolutions relating to the elimination of all forms of violence against women including the elimination of crimes against women committed in the name of honour and trafficking in women and girls.

41. Are there special procedures dealing with violence against women?

In March 1994, the Commission on Human Rights established the mandate, subsequently renewed every three years (the last time by the Human Rights Council in 2008), of a Special Rapporteur on violence against women, with the task to examine the causes and consequences of violence against women and to make recommendations. An important contribution by the Rapporteur was her report to the 57th Session of the Commission on Human Rights.[37] The report focused on 'violence against women perpetrated

and/or endorsed by the State during times of war (1997–2000)'. Numerous cases from thirteen countries are documented in the report. While recalling the continued and unabated violence against women, the report recorded the efforts of the International Criminal Tribunals for former Yugoslavia and for Rwanda (see Question 70) in facilitating the investigation and prosecution of such crimes, as well as those of the International Criminal Court, the Statute of which defines rape and other gender-based violence as crimes against humanity and war crimes. The subsequent report of the Special Rapporteur to the 58th Session of the Commission on Human Rights[38] focused on violence against women arising from cultural practices within the family, as they tend not to receive adequate attention and are often perceived as cultural practices that deserve tolerance and respect. Listed amongst the most disturbing of such practices are honour killings, pledging of girls for economic or cultural appeasement, discrimination or abuse stemming from caste practices, young/forced marriage and practices that violate women's reproductive rights. The Report identified the countries and regions where these practices occur as well as ideologies that perpetuate some cultural practices.

In his report to the 7th Session of the Human Rights Council[39], in 2008, the current Rapporteur elaborated on the need to develop transnational indicators on violence against women and on the response by the States to such violence.

42. Are the rights of the child protected by international human rights law?

September 1990, the Convention on the Rights of the Child (CRC) came into force, less than one year after it had been adopted by the United Nations General Assembly. By now a record number of States – more than 190 – have ratified the Convention.[40] States Parties to the Convention agree to take all appropriate measures to implement the rights recognized in the Convention. In doing so, they accept that the best interest of the child shall be the paramount consideration and guiding principle. The provisions are wide-ranging and include recognition of the importance of family

life for the child. They set minimum standards for health care, education, and legal, civil and social services.

The Convention is supplemented by two Optional Protocols adopted in 2000 and which entered into force in 2002: the Protocol on the involvement of children in armed conflict (see Question 45) and the Protocol on the sale of children, child prostitution and child pornography (see Question 44).

The International Labour Organization (ILO) has adopted several conventions on child labour: Convention No. 138 concerning Minimum Age for Admission to Employment (1973) and Convention No. 182 concerning the Prohibition and Immediate Action for the Elimination of the Worst Forms of Child Labour (1999).

43. How are the provisions of the Convention on the Rights of the Child (CRC) implemented?

The Committee on the Rights of the Child, established under the Convention and comprising independent experts, examines periodic reports submitted by States Parties on the implementation of the Convention. The Committee adopts concluding observations,

including suggestions and recommendations on each periodic report. These are transmitted to the State Party concerned and are intended to be widely publicized and serve as a basis for national debate on how to improve the enforcement of the provisions of the Convention. States' reports are examined in public sessions in which United Nations specialized agencies participate and are invited to submit information or advice on their areas of expertise. The Committee can transmit requests and indicate needs for technical advice or assistance arising from States' reports to the specialized agencies. The United Nations Children's Fund (UNICEF),[41] which plays an important role in promoting the Convention, is a significant participant in these proceedings. The Committee may recommend to the UN General Assembly that studies on specific issues relating to the rights of the child should be undertaken by the Secretary-General (see also Part II, Article 4).

44. What special procedures and instruments are there for the protection of children against sexual exploitation?

The Special Rapporteur of the Commission on Human Rights on the sale of children, child prostitution and child pornography has been operative since 1991 (the mandate was renewed by the Human Rights Council in 2008 for a period of three years). The work of the Special Rapporteur contributed to the elaboration of an Optional Protocol to the Convention on the Rights of the Child on the sale of children, child prostitution and child pornography, which was adopted by the UN General Assembly on 25 May 2000. The Protocol, which entered into force on 18 January 2002, calls on States to prohibit, by domestic legislation, the sale of children or their use for prostitution or pornography, whether such offences are committed domestically or transnationally, or on an individual or organized basis.[42]

A number of instruments exist for combating the trafficking of children and their use in sexual slavery:

• The Rome Statute of the International Criminal Court (adopted in 1998, in force since 2002) defines slavery and sexual slavery as crimes against humanity.

- ILO Convention No. 182 (adopted in 1999, in force since 2000) prohibits the use, procuring or offering of a child for prostitution and for the production of pornography or for pornographic performances. Illicit activities, in particular the production and trafficking of drugs, and work that, by its nature or the circumstances in which it is carried out, is likely to harm the health, safety or morals of children are also prohibited.
- The African Charter on the Rights and Welfare of the Child (adopted in 1990, in force since 1999) prohibits the sexual exploitation of children and their sale, trafficking and abduction.[43]
- The Optional Protocol to the United Nations Convention against Transnational Organized Crime (adopted in 2001, in force since 2003) provides for the prevention, suppression and punishment of trafficking in persons, especially women and children.

45. How are the rights of children protected in situations of armed conflict?

Since September 1997, a Special Representative of the Secretary-General on the use of children in armed conflict has been operative with the mandate to promote and protect the rights and welfare of children during every phase of armed conflict. On 12 February 2002, an Optional Protocol to the Convention on the Rights of the Child on the involvement of children in armed conflict came into force which prohibits States and non-state actors from using children (defined as under the age of 18) in armed conflicts.[44] While it does not prohibit the voluntary recruitment to the armed forces of children over 15 years of age, they cannot be forcibly conscripted or used in combat until the age of 18.

The protection of children in armed conflict is also provided for by the Rome Statute of the International Criminal Court (1998), which defines: (a) the conscription, enlistment and use in hostilities of children under 15 years by national armed forces or armed groups as war crimes; (b) the forcible transfer of children of a threatened ethnic, racial or religious group to another group

as genocide; and (c) rape, sexual slavery and enforced prostitution of children as war crimes.

ILO Convention No. 182, concerning the prohibition of child labour and immediate action for the elimination of its worst forms, prohibits the forced or compulsory recruitment of children under 18 years of age into armed conflict.

The African Charter on the Rights and Welfare of the Child prohibits the recruitment of children under 18 years of age into hostilities and their direct participation in internal strife.

An International Conference on War-Affected Children took place in September 2000 in Winnipeg, Canada, with the participation of representatives of governments, experts, academics, NGOs and young people. The conference adopted plans of action which, *inter alia*, called for wider adoption of international mechanisms; greater compliance, through such methods as increasing the accountability and ending the immunity of individuals involved in the use of children in armed conflict; the release of abducted children; an increase in humanitarian aid and assistance from the international community to deal with cases of children in armed conflict; and an increase in preventive measures.

On 13 November 2001, the General Assembly passed a resolution proclaiming the decade from 2001–2010 as the International Decade for a Culture of Peace and Non-Violence for the Children of the World.[45]

At an open debate in the Security Council on 20 November 2001 a Resolution[46] was adopted which notably underscores that individuals, 'entities' and corporations that maintain commercial relations with parties to conflicts should be held accountable if they promote or contribute to violations of the rights of children by parties to the conflict. All these issues were also discussed at the UN special session of the General Assembly on children in May 2002.

In July 2005, the Security Council, in its 1612 Resolution[47], decided to create the Security Council Working Group on Children and Armed Conflict (CAAC). The Working Group is entitled to review the reports of the monitoring and reporting mechanism (MRM), established by the same Resolution, make recommendations to the Council on possible measures to promote the protection of children affected by armed conflicts, and address requests, as

appropriate, to other bodies within the United Nations system for action to support implementation of Resolution 1612 in accordance with their respective mandates. The Monitoring and Reporting Mechanism seeks to monitor the following grave abuses: killing or maiming of children; recruiting or using child soldiers; attacks of Member States against schools or hospitals; rape and other grave sexual violence against children; abduction of children and denial of humanitarian access for children.

46. Does international law protect the rights of persons belonging to minorities?

Article 27 of the International Covenant on Civil and Political Rights and Article 30 of the Convention on the Rights of the Child both state that persons belonging to minorities shall not be denied the right to enjoy their own culture, practise their own religion or use their own language. The Human Rights Committee, which is the treaty body of the International Covenant on Civil and Political Rights (see Questions 12–17), has received complaints by individuals under the Optional Protocol relating to violations of Article 27.[48] Under the definition of 'racial discrimination', the International Convention on the Elimination of All Forms of Racial Discrimination includes national or ethnic origin (Article 1), thus forbidding discrimination on these grounds, as well as on the basis of race, colour and descent.

The most comprehensive United Nations human rights instrument devoted solely to minority rights is the Declaration on the Rights of Persons Belonging to National or Ethnic, Religious and Linguistic Minorities, which was adopted by consensus in 1992, by the United Nations General Assembly.[49] The Preamble to the Declaration states that the promotion and realization of the rights of persons belonging to minorities is an 'integral part of the development of society... within a democratic framework based on the rule of law...' Article 1 of the Declaration requires States to recognize and promote the identity of such minorities in community with other members of their group. Article 2 explicitly states the rights of persons belonging to minorities to enjoy their own culture, to practise their own religion and use their own language,

without interference or any form of discrimination. The General Assembly has appealed to States to 'take all the appropriate legislative and other measures to promote and give effect to the principles of the Declaration'.[50]

The Convention against Discrimination in Education (1960), adopted by the General Conference of UNESCO, specifically provides for the rights of national minorities with respect to their educational activities (Article 5), and forbids discrimination against any group of persons (Article 1).

47. How do the United Nations' human rights mechanisms address the issue of minorities?

The issue of minorities is long-standing, and was one of the reasons for the establishment, in 1947, of the Sub-Commission on Prevention of Discrimination and Protection of Minorities (later called the Sub-Commission on the Promotion and Protection of Human Rights), a subsidiary body of the Commission on Human Rights. The rights of persons belonging to ethnic, religious and linguistic minorities were the subject of several studies.[51] New approaches towards the implementation of effective international protection of minorities have been consistently pursued. In 1995, the Sub-Commission established a working group, which met annually and reported to the Commission on Human Rights. The working group was mandated to examine possible situations where minorities might face problems and to develop strategies for protecting their rights. The working group submitted a Statement to the World Conference against Racism focusing on the relationship between the elimination of racial discrimination and the protection of minorities.

In 2006, the Sub-Commission was replaced by the Human Rights Council Advisory Committee, which had its first session in August 2008.

The mandate of the Independent Expert on Minority Issues, appointed by the Commission on Human Rights in 2005, was renewed by the Human Rights Council in 2008, for three years.

In addition, the Human Rights Council established, in 2007, a Forum on Minority Issues. The Forum provides a platform for promoting dialogue and cooperation on issues related to national or ethnic, religious and linguistic minorities. The Forum is also authorized to identify and analyse best practices, challenges, opportunities and initiatives for the further implementation of the Declaration on the Rights of Persons Belonging to National or Ethnic, Religious and Linguistic Minorities.

48. Why is the issue of the protection of minorities considered more important today than it was in the past?

During the past decades, the question of minority rights has become a major issue of global concern due to the proliferation of violent internal conflicts, with consequent massive costs in human suffering, displacement of people, and economic and social disruption. Ongoing, seemingly intractable, internal conflicts in Africa, Asia and Latin America were augmented by new conflicts, arising from the dissolution of the former Soviet Union and the disintegration of the former Yugoslavia, with the abhorrent 'ethnic cleansing' which accompanied the latter.

Many of these conflicts have their roots in long-standing grievances and discrimination of minorities. Resultant assertions of identity, often politically manipulated, are expressed in claims to self-determination. The denial of these claims and the absence of mechanisms to deal with them often result in violent conflict and even civil war.

In *An Agenda For Peace*,[52] Boutros Boutros-Ghali, the former Secretary-General of the United Nations, pointed out that, in spite of the growing 'cooperation of both regional and continental associations of States, fierce new assertions of nationalism and sovereignty spring up, and the cohesion of States is threatened by brutal ethnic, religious, social, cultural or linguistic strife'. He also stated that 'one requirement for solutions to these problems lies in commitment to human rights with a special sensitivity to those of minorities, whether ethnic, religious, social or linguistic'.

In his *Millennium Report*, in 2000, Kofi Annan, the UN Secretary-General at that time, pointed out that most conflicts happen especially in those countries 'which are badly governed or where power and wealth are very unfairly distributed between ethnic or religious groups. So the best way to prevent conflict is promote political arrangements in which all groups are fairly represented, combined with human rights, minority rights and broad-based economic development.'[53]

49. What measures have been taken at the regional level to protect persons belonging to minorities?

The Conference for Security and Cooperation in Europe (now the Organization for Security and Cooperation in Europe – OSCE; see Questions 102–103)[54] appointed a High Commissioner on National Minorities in December 1992, as a conflict-prevention mechanism. The High Commissioner's function is to provide early warning and early action, as appropriate, in regard to tensions involving national minority issues. The High Commissioner is allowed free access to the territory of any participating State and may receive information directly from various sources including non-governmental organizations. This institution has proven to be a valuable instrument in facilitating discussion and dialogue between conflicting parties and helping to prevent and resolve disputes related to the existence of ethnic minorities.

At sub-regional levels, developments in relation to the human rights of minorities have been pursued by various sub-regional bodies, such as the Council of Baltic States, the Central European Initiative, the Commonwealth of Independent States and the League of Arab States.

In February 1995, the Council of Europe adopted the Framework Convention for the Protection of National Minorities. This represents the first legally binding, multilateral instrument devoted to the protection of national minorities. The Convention, which came into force on 1 February 1998, covers many areas, such as the right to linguistic freedom and education, and participation in public life.

Furthermore, the European Charter for Regional or Minority Languages, in force since 1 March 1998, laid down a series of educational, administrative and judicial measures, based on the recognition that the right to use a minority language in private and public life is an inalienable right.

Other activities, undertaken by the European Council on Racial Equality (ECRE), include 'group' specific activities, such as the Specialist Group on the Roma, and 'subject' specific activities, which address such issues as racism and intolerance in Member States.

50. What international instruments have been elaborated to ensure the rights of indigenous peoples?

There are at least 370 million indigenous people in around seventy States, in all parts of the world. It is the common experience of indigenous peoples worldwide that a high proportion of them live below the poverty line. They have the shortest life expectancy and the highest infant mortality rates, the poorest school retention and graduation rates, and the highest unemployment figures. Most of them live in overcrowded, poor quality housing and suffer endemic environmental health problems.

The main international, legally binding instrument that exists to protect the rights of indigenous peoples is the International Labour Organization Convention No. 169 concerning Indigenous and Tribal Peoples in Independent Countries, adopted in June 1989, and which entered into force in September 1991.[55] It affirms that no State or social group has the right to deny the identity of indigenous peoples, and places responsibility on States for ensuring, with the participation of indigenous peoples, their rights and integrity.

A major step towards the recognition of the rights of indigenous peoples was the adoption, by the General Assembly of the United Nations, of the Declaration on the Rights of Indigenous Peoples (13 September 2007). It sets out the individual and collective rights of the indigenous peoples (right to culture, education, health, identity, language, employment and others). The principles

of non-discrimination and the right to self-determination are also included in the Declaration.

51. What other action is being taken to promote the rights of indigenous peoples?

The United Nations Working Group on Indigenous Populations, created in 1982 by the Sub-Commission on Human Rights, was unique and formed the centre of indigenous rights activities within the United Nations system. It functioned as a forum attended annually by 500 to 600 indigenous representatives who exchanged views in a free and democratic manner with governments, non-governmental organizations, United Nations specialized agencies and other interested parties. The Working Group reported annually to the Sub-Commission on the Promotion and Protection of Human Rights and the Commission on Human Rights. The Human Rights Council replaced the Working Group in December 2007, with an Expert Mechanism on the Rights of Indigenous Peoples. Composed of five experts, this Expert Mechanism is authorized to provide thematic expertise on the rights of indigenous peoples to the Human Rights Council. The Expert Mechanism held its first session in October 2008 and its first study is devoted to the right of indigenous peoples to education.

The United Nations Economic and Social Council established, in 2000, the Permanent Forum on Indigenous Issues (UNPFII).[56] The Permanent Forum is composed of sixteen members, eight of whom are indigenous experts. The mandate of the Forum is to address indigenous issues related to economic and social development, culture, the environment, education, health and human rights. This includes providing expert advice and recommendations on indigenous issues to ECOSOC and promoting the integration and coordination of activities relating to indigenous issues within the United Nations system. The Permanent Forum held its first session from 13 to 24 May 2002 in New York at the United Nations Headquarters.

In 2001, the Commission on Human Rights appointed, for a period of three years, a Special Rapporteur on the situation of human rights and fundamental freedoms of indigenous people (the

Rapporteur's mandate was renewed by the Human Rights Council in 2007, for a period of three years).[57] The mandate of the Special Rapporteur includes formulating recommendations and proposals on the appropriate measures and activities to prevent and remedy violations of the human rights and fundamental freedoms of indigenous people. The Special Rapporteur also seeks constructive cooperation with the Working Group on Indigenous Populations (now the Expert Mechanism) and the Permanent Forum on Indigenous Issues, and forges close working relationships with other mandate holders of the Special Procedures of the Human Rights Council. The Special Rapporteur's first report to the Commission on Human Rights identified major human rights issues affecting indigenous people. These were: land rights; homelands and territories; education and culture; poverty; social organization and customary legal systems; political representation; and autonomy and self-determination.

Treaty bodies have also considered the rights of indigenous peoples. The Committee on the Elimination of Racial Discrimination (CERD) (see Questions 32–34), has considered the situation of indigenous peoples in relation to discrimination. The Human Rights Committee (see Questions 14–16) has examined cases brought by indigenous persons alleging violation of their rights under Article 27 of the International Covenant on Civil and Political Rights, which promotes cultural rights of persons belonging to ethnic, religious or linguistic minorities.

The United Nations General Assembly had proclaimed the ten years starting from December 1994 as the Decade of the World's Indigenous People.[58] The goal of the Decade was to strengthen international cooperation towards the solution of problems faced by indigenous peoples and to generate greater respect for cultural diversity. On 22 December 2004, the General Assembly decided to proclaim the Second International Decade of the World's Indigenous People, starting from January 2005.[59] The Decade has five main objectives: promoting non-discrimination, as well as full and effective participation of indigenous peoples in programmes and decisions that directly or indirectly affect them, redefining culturally appropriate development policies, developing strong monitoring mechanisms and enhancing accountability at the international,

regional and national level for the implementation of legal, policy and operational frameworks for protection of indigenous peoples.

52. What international instruments and procedures are there for the protection of migrant workers?

The increase of migration in recent decades is of great concern to the international community. The ILO estimates that there are more than 100 million migrant workers and members of their families worldwide. The vulnerability of migrants, particularly as a result of increasing manifestations of discrimination, racism and xenophobia against them, is of major concern.

There are a number of principles and standards set out within the framework of the ILO system providing protection for migrants at work. These include: the Convention concerning Migration for Employment (No. 97), the Convention concerning Migrations in Abusive Conditions and the Promotion of Equality of Opportunity and Treatment of Migrant Workers (No. 143), the Recommendation concerning Migration for Employment (No. 86) the Recommendation concerning Migrant Workers (No. 151), and the Resolution concerning a fair deal for migrant workers in a global economy (ILO General Conference 2004).

A comprehensive instrument, the International Convention on the Protection of the Rights of All Migrant Workers and Members of their Families, was adopted in December 1990 by the General Assembly of the United Nations. The Convention came into force on 1 July 2003.

A Committee was established to monitor the implementation of the Convention and to receive individual complaints of alleged violations of the Convention.

The Convention applies not only to migrant workers who have legal entitlement to work within a country, but to all those who are illegally working in the States Parties as well, and includes a number of different types of migrant worker, such as 'seasonal workers', 'itinerant workers' and 'self-employed workers'. It does not include persons employed by international organizations or foreign governments, or students, trainees, refugees or stateless persons.

The Special Rapporteur on the human rights of migrants, appointed in 1999 by the Commission on Human Rights, has drawn the Commission's attention to the abuse suffered by migrants and expressed particular concern about family disruption and trafficking in persons. The irregular situation created by the above is often passed on to the children of migrants, who in turn risk becoming stateless. The Rapporteur's mandate was recently renewed (in 2008) by the Human Rights Council for a period of three years.

53. How are the rights of persons with disabilities protected?

The question of the protection of the rights of persons with disabilities gained prominence in the UN agenda since the proclamation by the General Assembly of the year 1981 as the 'International Year of the Disabled' under the slogan 'Full Participation and Equality'. The goals of the international year were to secure prevention of disability, rehabilitation to the disabled and full integration of the disabled in society.

In 1993, the World Conference on Human Rights reaffirmed that 'all human rights and fundamental freedoms are universal, and thus unreservedly include persons with disabilities' (Vienna Declaration and Programme of Action, A/CONF.157/23, para. 63 of the Declaration).

On 13 December 2006, the General Assembly adopted the Convention on the Rights of Persons with Disabilities and its Optional Protocol. Both entered into force on 3 May 2008. The Convention aims to ensure that persons with disabilities enjoy human rights on an equal basis with others. The Convention adopts a broad categorization of persons with disabilities and identifies areas where adaptations need to be made for persons with disabilities to effectively exercise their rights. It refers to civil and political rights of persons with disabilities (such as the right to marry and form a family), as well as to economic, social and cultural rights (such as the right to enjoy an adequate standard of living). According to the provisions of the Convention, the States Parties must, *inter alia*, ensure recognition before the law of all persons with disabilities; put in place laws and take all the necessary measures to

protect these persons from exploitation, violence and abuse. They must also promote the personal mobility of disabled persons and ensure that they are not deprived of their liberty because of their disability. Regarding education, the States must ensure the inclusion of students with disabilities in the general education system and their equal access to vocational training, adult education and lifelong learning.

An important element introduced by the Convention is the issue of accessibility. The States Parties must develop minimum standards of accessibility of facilities and services open to the public (such as transportation, information and communication) in order to ensure, for the persons with disabilities, the equal enjoyment of related rights.

The Protocol recognizes the competence of the Committee, established under the Convention, to receive and consider individual complaints regarding violations of the rights enshrined in the Convention.[60] The Committee held its first session on 23-27 February 2009.

At the regional level, the Inter-American Convention on the Elimination of All Forms of Discrimination against Persons with Disabilities was adopted in 1999 and came into force in September 2001.[61] The Convention establishes a Committee to review the reports of the States Parties on the application of the Convention.

54. How does international law protect refugees?

International and internal conflict, as well as internal strife, force people to leave their homes in an attempt to save their lives and to escape massive violations of their human rights. If they move within their own country, they are called internally displaced persons. Those who leave their country are called refugees.

The Convention relating to the Status of Refugees (1951) and its Protocol (1966)[62] recognize as refugees only those who leave their country because of a 'well-founded fear of being persecuted for reasons of race, religion, nationality, membership of a particular social group or political opinion' and are unable, or owing to

such fear, are unwilling to return (Article 1 of the Convention). The security of refugees rests on being granted asylum and on the observance of the principle of *non-refoulement*, which means that no person should be faced with expulsion or compulsory return, either at the border or after having entered another country, to a country where his or her life or freedom may be threatened because of the reasons enumerated above. The Convention stipulates that refugees should have the same rights as those accorded to nationals and at least the same as those accorded to other aliens. The Convention Against Torture (see Questions 26–27) reinforces the principle of *non-refoulement* in the case of persons in danger of being subjected to torture (Article 3). The right to asylum is not yet codified universally, although the right to seek and enjoy asylum is recognized in the Universal Declaration of Human Rights (Article 14). The regional instruments that exist, are the Conventions adopted by the Organisation of American States[63] (see Questions 99–100 and Part II, Article 14) and the OAU Convention Governing the Specific Aspects of Refugee Problems in Africa (see Question 95).

55. What are the responsibilities of the United Nations High Commissioner for Refugees (UNHCR)?

The United Nations High Commissioner for Refugees (UNHCR) is responsible for supervising international provisions for the protection of refugees and for seeking durable solutions by assisting governments to facilitate the voluntary repatriation of refugees and/or their integration within new national communities.

In 1951, when the UNHCR was established, there were an estimated 1 million refugees. At the end of 2007 there were 16 million refugees spread over five continents, who were 'of concern' to the UNHCR. These included refugees and other groups such as refugees returning home but needing help to rebuild their lives, local civilian communities affected by the movements of refugees and internally displaced persons. All of these groups were receiving assistance from the UNHCR. While internally displaced persons are not protected by international law or eligible to receive many types of aid, an estimated 13.7 million of these people receive help from

the UNHCR under the general provisions of human rights law and humanitarian law, on an *ad hoc* operational basis. This protection is similar to that provided to refugees.[64] The UNHCR is increasingly concerned with the root causes of conflicts and with the need for 'early-warning' and 'preventative strategies to avert and resolve refugee flows and internal displacement'. According to the United Nations High Commissioner for Refugees, preventative strategies required a comprehensive approach, encompassing development assistance, as well as humanitarian action and the protection of human rights'.[65]

The overwhelming political changes and new patterns of conflict over the past decade have caused new challenges in this regard. To confront the dynamic and changing environment, UNHCR launched the 'Global Consultations on International Protection' in 2001. This led to the elaboration of the 'Agenda for Protection'. Premised on the Declaration adopted by States Parties to the 1951 Convention and/or its 1967 Protocol on the occasion of the Convention's fiftieth anniversary, the Agenda focuses on activities to strengthen international protection of refugees and asylum-seekers.

56. What role do non-governmental organizations (NGOs) play in the protection of refugees?

Since its inception the UNHCR has worked with a large number of national and international NGOs. Their activities include emergency relief work, long-term development, human rights monitoring and advocacy. UNHCR Statutes explicitly provide for UNHCR assistance to refugees to be administered through private as well as public agencies. In 1994, UNHCR cooperation with NGOs expanded through what is known as the 'Partnership in Action' process, which was reviewed in 2000. Some 50 per cent of all UNHCR programmes are now implemented by international NGOs and about 20%–25% of its entire budget is spent on aid to refugees through more than 800 NGOs. The cooperation agreements between UNHCR and NGOs concern assistance to refugees and other persons of concern in such areas as health,

nutrition, water supply, sanitation, community development, education, site construction and maintenance.

57. What regional instruments have been adopted for the protection of refugees?

The most comprehensive regional instrument is the Convention Governing the Specific Aspects of Refugee Problems in Africa, adopted by the Organization of African Unity (see Questions 95–98) in 1969, and which entered into force in 1974.[66] This Convention expands the definition of the term 'refugee' in comparison with the 1951 Convention. The expanded definition applies to every person who is compelled to seek refuge outside his or her country of origin or citizenship for reasons including external aggression, occupation and internal civil disturbance.

This expanded mandate also applies to the 1984 Cartagena Declaration on Refugees, adopted by the Central American States, joined by Mexico and Panama, as well as to the revised text of the Bangkok Principles on the Status and Treatment of Refugees (originally adopted in 1966), which was adopted by the Asian-African Legal Consultative Organization in 2001.

58. How is the issue of internally displaced persons addressed?

The problem of internally displaced persons (IDPs) gained new urgency during the 1990s, partly because of the scale of displacement caused by new internal conflicts during the decade[67], and it still remains a topic of human rights concern.

In 1992, in response to growing international concern, the United Nations Secretary-General, at the request of the Commission on Human Rights, appointed a Special Representative on Internally Displaced Persons to analyse the causes of internal displacement; ascertain the needs of IDPs; propose measures to protect them; and seek solutions for internal displacement. The Special Representative has formulated a set of standards entitled Guiding Principles on Internal Displacement, based on international human rights law,

humanitarian law and refugee law, thus identifying the various provisions of existing international law applicable to IDPs. The Principles recognize that governments are the principal actors in the protection of internally displaced persons. The Principles set out guidelines to: encourage governments to provide fair and equal treatment to IDPs; minimize the occurrence of situations that lead to internal displacement; and ensure safe and dignified return for resettlement and reintegration. The Special Representative has also drawn attention to the plight of IDPs in areas not under government control, where they are subject to the actions of non-state actors and where humanitarian access is blocked. The Principles mark the first set of standards spelling out what protection should mean for the internally displaced. While not binding, governments and the appropriate United Nations bodies are urged to further the implementation of these Principles. The Representative's mandate was renewed in 2007 by the Human Rights Council for three years.

59. Is there an international code for the treatment of persons deprived of their liberty?

In 1955, the First United Nations Congress on the Prevention of Crime and Treatment of Offenders adopted Standard Minimum Rules for the Treatment of Prisoners. They were subsequently amended and approved by ECOSOC in 1957 and in 1977. The purpose of these rules was not to describe in detail a model for penitentiary systems but to establish principles and standards in respect to the treatment of prisoners. In 1979 the United Nations General Assembly adopted a Code of Conduct for Law Enforcement Officials and, in 1988, a Body of Principles for the Protection of All Persons under Any Form of Detention or Imprisonment. In 1990, the eleven-point Basic Principles for the Treatment of Prisoners were adopted (Resolution 45/111 of the General Assembly) in order to promote the full implementation of the rights of prisoners. Accordingly, all prisoners are entitled to the human rights set out in the Universal Declaration of Human Rights and the International Covenants allowing only those restrictions that are necessitated by the fact of incarceration. In particular, prisoners shall have the

right to take part in cultural activities and education, and shall have access to health services without discrimination due to their legal situation.

The General Assembly also adopted codes of conduct for the protection of juveniles deprived of their liberty (Resolution 45/11 of 14 December 1990) and for the protection of persons who are mentally ill (Resolution 46/111 of 17 December 1991).

Although none of these instruments is legally binding, all of them are important guides for States in the treatment of persons deprived of their liberty.

60. What instruments and procedures are there for the protection of human rights defenders?

On 9 December 1998 the General Assembly of the United Nations, by Resolution 53/144, adopted the Declaration on the Right and Responsibility of Individuals, Groups and Organs of Society to Promote and Protect Universally Recognized Human Rights and Fundamental Freedoms, generally referred to as the 'Declaration on Human Rights Defenders'. The Declaration reaffirms, clarifies and strengthens recognized legal norms relating to the work of human rights defenders and acknowledges their role in promoting and protecting human rights. Moreover it provides an important normative basis for effective implementation and protection of human rights standards. Human rights defenders have the right to raise money for this purpose and the right to criticize and protest against violations of human rights. The Declaration calls upon States to actively promote and protect human rights defenders by legislation and other action.

In its Resolution 2000/61, the Commission on Human Rights commented 'that in many countries persons and organisations engaged in promoting and defending human rights and fundamental freedoms are often subjected to threats, harassment, insecurity, arbitrary detention and extra-judicial execution'. The resolution, furthermore, requested the Secretary-General to appoint a Special Representative to report on the situation of human rights defenders in all parts of the world and on possible means to enhance

their protection, in compliance with the Declaration. The Special Representative, who was appointed for an initial period of three years, may seek, receive, examine and respond to information on the situation of anyone who is engaged in promoting and defending human rights, in order to establish dialogue with governments and others to promote the implementation of the Declaration, and to recommend effective strategies to better protect human rights defenders. The Special Representative, in reporting to the 58th Session of the Commission on Human Rights (2002), reflected that the numerous communications alleging serious violations of the rights of human rights defenders, received during the past year, underlined 'the continuous need for the effective promotion and protection of the rights of human rights defenders.'

In March 2008 the Human Rights Council appointed, instead of the Special Representative of the Secretary-General, a Special Rapporteur on the situation of human rights defenders.

Procedures for the promotion and protection of human rights

61. Can an appeal be made to the United Nations if a person feels that his/her human rights are being or have been violated?

The United Nations has received hundreds of thousands of complaints from individuals and organizations concerning alleged violations of human rights. Since the introduction of a special procedure on this matter (see Question 65), the number of complaints has grown significantly. Various procedures have been developed for the Commission on Human Rights and the Human Rights Council, which replaced it in 2006, to deal with complaints about gross violations of human rights. There are also treaty-based procedures which allow individual cases to be considered by the Human Rights

Committee (see Question 16), the Committee on Economic, Social and Cultural Rights (see Question 19) the Committee on the Elimination of Racial Discrimination (CERD) (see Question 33), the Committee Against Torture (see Question 27), the Committee on the Elimination of All Forms of Discrimination Against Women (CEDAW) (see Question 36), the Committee on the Protection of All Migrant Workers and Members of Their Families (see Question 52) and the Committee on Enforced Disappearances (see Question 30), when operative. UNESCO and ILO have also established individual

complaints procedures pertaining to alleged violations of human rights within their respective fields of competence (see Questions 77 and 80 respectively).

62. What procedures were developed to bring complaints concerning human rights violations before the Commission on Human Rights?

The Commission on Human Rights (replaced by the Human Rights Council in 2006) was the body primarily responsible within the United Nations for dealing with human rights issues, including complaints alleging violations of human rights.

When the Commission was established, no provision was made for machinery whereby individuals or groups could seek redress for alleged violations of human rights. A procedure (ECOSOC Resolution 728F of 1959) was developed later on, which permitted the drafting of two lists of communications from the complaints received: a non-confidential list dealing with general issues relating to the protection and promotion of human rights, and a confidential list made up of complaints against States.

With regard to the non-confidential part of the procedure, a landmark was reached in 1967, when ECOSOC adopted Resolution 1235, empowering the Commission on Human Rights to 'make a thorough study [on the basis of information received] of situations which reveal a consistent pattern of violations of human rights, as exemplified by the policy of apartheid', and to report and make recommendations to ECOSOC. Fact-finding studies were then initiated and a Working Group of Experts on Southern Africa was set up in 1967. Subsequently, a group with a mandate to look into alleged violations of human rights in the occupied Arab territories and an *ad hoc* Working Group on Chile (terminated in 1979) were created. Political will and agreement on these situations allowed the Commission on Human Rights to pursue its mandate to consider publicly situations concerning violations of human rights and fundamental freedoms in any part of the world.

The confidential procedure was formalized in 1970 by ECOSOC Resolution 1503 (XLVIII), so that 'a consistent pattern

of gross and reliably attested violations of human rights and fundamental freedoms', occurring in any country of the world, could be examined. For the first time, communications could be submitted, not only by victims of violations, but also by any person or group or non-governmental organization with a direct and reliable knowledge of the violations. This confidential procedure was revised by ECOSOC Resolution 2000/3. Under the revised procedure, the complaints, together with any replies received from governments, were examined, in the first instance, by the Working Group on Communications of the Sub-Commission on the Promotion and Protection of Human Rights. The Group decided whether or not to refer a case to the second stage of the procedure, i.e. to the Working Group on Situations of the Commission on Human Rights. The Working Group could forward a situation to the Commission, in which case it usually made specific recommendations for action. The Commission could decide either to discontinue the consideration of a situation, to keep the situation under review and appoint an independent expert, or to discontinue the consideration of the matter under the confidential procedure in order to take it up under the public procedure established by ESOCOC Resolution 1235 (XLII). All material provided by individuals and governments, as well as the decisions taken at the various stages of the procedure, remained confidential and were not made public. Unlike other similar procedures, there was no provision for urgent measures of protection.

The Commission publicly announced the names of the countries that had been considered under the Resolution 1503 procedure[68] at its session of the same year, as well as those of countries no longer dealt with under the procedure. The effectiveness of this procedure depended largely upon the voluntary cooperation of States. It had an important function in that it embraced all rights recognized in the Universal Declaration of Human Rights and the International Covenants, and was applied to all Member States of the United Nations. It thus complemented other treaty-based procedures that were applicable only to States Parties to those treaties.

In June 2007 the Human Rights Council (which replaced the Commission on Human Rights in 2006) adopted Resolution 5/1,

by which a new Complaints Procedure was established to reform Procedure 1503 (see Question 63).

63. What are the main features of the Human Rights Council?

The General Assembly, by its Resolution 60/251 of 3 April 2006, decided to create a Human Rights Council (HRC) in order to replace the Commission on Human Rights. It is a subsidiary body of the General Assembly, unlike the Commission, which was a subsidiary body of the ECOSOC. The HRC is composed of 47 members. The members are elected directly by the majority of the members of the General Assembly. The Member States of the HRC are required to uphold the highest standards in the promotion and protection of human rights. Furthermore, the Membership in the Council of a country which commits gross and systematic violations of human rights may be suspended by two-thirds majority vote of the Council. The distribution of seats among regional groups is made according to the principle of equitable geographical representation.[69]

In June 2007, one year after its first meeting, and in compliance with General Assembly resolution 60/251, the Human Rights Council adopted Resolution 5/1, which assembled a package of elements establishing the procedures, mechanisms and structures for its future work, including the setting up of a new Complaints Procedure 'to address consistent patterns of gross and reliably attested violations of all human rights and all fundamental freedoms occurring in any part of the world and under any circumstances'. The new Complaints Procedure, based on Procedure 1503, was improved where necessary to ensure that it would be impartial, objective, efficient, victims-oriented and conducted in a timely manner. It retains its confidential nature, with a view to enhancing cooperation with the State concerned.

The Council's agenda and programme of work provides the opportunity to discuss all thematic human rights issues and situations that require the Council's attention throughout the year. The Human Rights Council has assumed all functions of the Commission on Human Rights as well as important new ones,

including the coordination and mainstreaming of human rights within the United Nations system, making recommendations to the General Assembly for the further development of international law in the field of human rights and the conducting of the Universal Periodic Review (see Question 68).

An Advisory Committee, replacing the Sub-Commission on the Promotion and Protection of Human Rights, was established to support the Council's work. Functioning as a think tank, the Committee provides expertise and advice and conducts substantive research and studies on thematic issues of interest to the Council at its request.

64. What initiatives have been taken by the Commission on Human Rights and by the Human Rights Council to deal with human rights violations?

Gradually, since 1979, and on an *ad hoc* basis, a range of supervisory mechanisms have been developed. They do not derive their legitimacy from any particular human rights instrument. They each have their own particular mandate and were established by resolutions of the Human Rights Commission, as approved by the ECOSOC. Essentially mechanisms of implementation, these special procedures aimed to promote compliance by governments with human rights standards. These mechanisms, known collectively as the 'Special Procedures' of the Commission on Human Rights and, now, of the Human Rights Council, fall into two groups: those addressing human rights issues by theme on a global basis and those which focus on the overall human rights situation in a specific country.

These mechanisms have different titles such as Special Rapporteur, Special Representative, Independent Expert or Working Group. Members of the Working Groups and the individuals appointed as rapporteurs, representatives or independent experts, serve in their personal capacity and do not receive any remuneration. In addition to the above, the Secretary-General may be requested to prepare reports, which may be either thematic or country-based.

65. What are the 'special procedures' of the Commission on Human Rights now assumed by the Human Rights Council?

The special procedures and the practice of appointing Special Rapporteurs and Working Groups, established by the Commission of Human Rights, were assumed by the Human Rights Council. All thematic mandates have been renewed and some new ones have been added, such as the mandate on access to safe drinking water and sanitation.

The first of the thematic procedures was established in 1980 and was called the Working Group on Enforced or Involuntary Disappearances. Its primary role was to act as an intermediary between families of missing persons and governments with the aim of clarifying the location of the missing persons. In pursuing this aim, the Working Group analyses cases of disappeared persons; receives information from governmental and non-governmental sources; transmits cases to the governments concerned, with the request that they carry out investigations, and relays governments' replies to the families of the disappeared. It also examines allegations of a general nature concerning specific countries, and intervenes with governments when relatives of missing persons, or people who have cooperated with the Group, have suffered intimidation or reprisals as a result. Impunity has been identified as the major reason for disappearance, thus underlying the importance of holding perpetrators accountable for their crimes. The Working Group elaborates general conclusions and recommendations, which are included in its report to the Human Rights Council (see Question 63).[70] In 2008, the HRC renewed the Working Group's mandate for three years.

The Working Group on Arbitrary Detention was established in 1991, by the Commission on Human Rights, and was mandated to investigate cases of detention imposed arbitrarily, or otherwise inconsistent with relevant international standards, accepted by the States concerned. Since 1997, the mandate of the Group has been extended to include the issues of administrative custody of asylum seekers and immigrants. Cases are received and considered within the framework of a 'complaints mechanism'. After consideration the Working Group adopts 'opinions' on individual cases, which are transmitted to the government concerned. Where the working

group finds detention of an individual to be arbitrary, the government is asked to take the necessary steps to remedy the situation (see also Part II, Article 9). In 2007, the Human Rights Council renewed the Working Group's mandate for three years.

The mandate of the Special Rapporteur on Extrajudicial, Summary or Arbitrary Executions (see also Part II, Article 3) was established in 1982, and in 1985 that of a Special Rapporteur on Torture (see Question 28) was also established. All four of the above mechanisms have an urgent action procedure, whereby they can promptly react to situations of concern by requesting that governments take immediate action to rectify or clarify a case.

Other 'special procedures' include the Rapporteurs (or Special Representatives) on Internally Displaced Persons (see Question 58); the Sale of Children, Child Prostitution and Child Pornography (see Question 44); Children in Armed Conflict (see Question 45); Independence of Judges and Lawyers (see Part II, Article 10); Elimination of Violence against Women (see Question 41); Contemporary Forms of Racism, Racial Discrimination, Xenophobia and Related Intolerance (see Questions 34 and 35 and Part II, Article 2); Religious Intolerance (see Part II, Article 18); Freedom of Opinion and Expression (see Part II, Article 19); Human Rights Defenders (see Question 60); Indigenous People (see Questions 50–51); Mercenaries as a Means of Impeding the Exercise of the Right of Peoples to Self-determination; Minority Issues; Contemporary Forms of Slavery; Human Rights and International Solidarity; Promotion and Protection of Human Rights while Countering Terrorism; Trafficking in Persons, especially Women and Children; and Human Rights and Transnational Corporations and other Business Enterprises.

Thematic mandates relating to economic, social and cultural rights include: the right to education; housing; food; health; human rights and extreme poverty as well as the right to development (see also Questions 114–115); access to safe drinking water and sanitation; structural adjustment and foreign debt. In 2008, with resolution 7/4, the Human Rights Council decided to merge the last two mandates and established the post of the 'Independent Expert on the effects of foreign debt and other related international financial obligations of States on the full enjoyment of all human rights, particularly economic, social and cultural rights'.

As of May 2009, under the country mandates, eight countries[71] were under scrutiny by Special Rapporteurs reporting to the United Nations General Assembly and to the Human Rights Council. Furthermore, situations in some countries were examined by Special Rapporteurs, reporting only to the Commission on Human Rights, and later the Human Rights Council.[72]

66. What are the working methods related to the 'special procedures'?

All those who are charged with carrying out the special procedures are mandated to research or examine the issues of concern, in terms of effective implementation of international human rights standards. In doing so, they may objectively seek and receive information from governmental and non-governmental sources, including victims of human rights violations, and ask governments to comment on information on specific cases. They also undertake on-site country visits, with the consent of the State concerned, for more intensive examination of either a specific case or the overall situation. Their aim is to establish constructive dialogue with governments and to recommend to them ways to improve human rights protection. Moreover, several mandates require their holders to deal with non-State entities, particularly in strife-torn situations. A growing number of mandates now address international institutions, in order to consider the impact of their policies on human rights. Special Rapporteurs and Working Groups have renewable mandates (up to a maximum of six years). They include in their detailed reports to the UN General Assembly and the Human Rights Council general conclusions indicating the gravity and nature of the human rights situations covered by their mandates and recommendations for further action. Field Officers may be used in connection with certain mandates.[73]

At the twelfth Annual Meeting of special procedures mandate holders in 2005, it was agreed to establish a Coordination Committee. The Committee's main function is to coordinate the work among the mandate holders and to act as a bridge between them and the OHCHR, the broader UN human rights framework, and civil society.

67. What is the importance of the 'special procedures' for the promotion and protection of human rights?

The overall significance of the special procedures is that they reflect an evolution in human rights activities, from an earlier focus on standard-setting to one on implementation and compliance with established standards. A framework of procedures and mechanisms for the protection and realization of human rights is thus being established. To be the focus of some special procedure is an indication of grave human rights violations, and States lobby assiduously against such exposure and public censure. Public scrutiny of a State's practices and mistreatment of its citizens can in itself act as a protective measure, preventing further abuses and saving lives. Urgent action procedures may impede further violations. Maintaining international pressure and disapproval can result in States improving their human rights situation.

Success ultimately depends upon the responsiveness of States and thus upon their sensitivity to public scrutiny and to remaining on the public agenda of the Council and General Assembly.

68. How does the Universal Periodic Review Mechanism contribute to the promotion of human rights?

An innovation introduced with the creation of the Human Rights Council, is the Universal Periodic Review (UPR) Mechanism, which according to the UN Secretary-General Ban Ki-moon 'has the potential to promote and protect human rights in the darkest corners of the world'.[74] The aim is to draw attention of the UN Member States to their responsibility to fully respect and protect human rights.

The Universal Periodic Review is one of the key elements of the institution-building package[75], agreed to by the Council on 18 June 2007. It is the review of the human rights record of all 192 UN Member States, starting with the Member States of the HRC. According to the Human Rights Council Mandate, this procedure should ensure 'universality of coverage and equal treatment with

respect to all States'.[76] The UPR involves assessing States' human rights situations, addressing human rights violations, providing technical assistance to States in order to enhance their capacity to meet their human rights obligations and sharing best practices in the field of human rights among States and other stakeholders.

According to the UPR Mechanism, all UN Member States are reviewed every four years (48 States per year). The Members of the Human Rights Council are reviewed during their term of membership. The reviews are conducted by the UPR Working Group and each State review is assisted by three members of the Human Rights Council, known as a 'troika', who serve as Rapporteurs. The review takes place in a discussion during a UPR Working Group meeting. The State concerned answers questions. Following the discussion, its summary in a form of a report is prepared by the 'troika', with the involvement of the State under review and with the assistance of the Office of the High Commissioner for Human Rights (OHCHR). The State concerned has the opportunity to make comments on the recommendations and the final report has to be adopted at a plenary session of the Human Rights Council.

The reviews are based on information provided by the State under review, reports by the Special Procedures holders (see Question 66), reports by the UN human rights treaty bodies and other UN bodies and agencies and information from other stakeholders, including national human rights institutions. Under the Universal Periodic Review Mechanism, NGOs can submit reports and can take part in the discussions during the Working Group meetings.

The First UPR Working Group Session was held in April 2008. As of May 2009, more than one third of the UN Member States had been reviewed.

Protection of human rights in times of armed conflict and responses to systematic and gross violations of human rights

69. How does international law protect human rights in times of armed conflict?

Even in periods of armed conflict, protection of basic human rights of civilians and combatants should be ensured and this is the subject of international humanitarian law.

The history of international humanitarian law is closely associated with that of the Red Cross. The Red Cross (today known as the International Committee of the Red Cross and Red Crescent Movement, ICRC) arose out of the work of Henri Dunant, a Swiss humanitarian, who organized emergency aid services at the battle of Solferino in 1859.

The Geneva Convention of 1864, the first multilateral agreement on humanitarian law, committed governments to take care of the war wounded, whether enemy or friend. This Convention was extended by the Hague Conventions of 1899 and 1907 and the Geneva Conventions of 1906 and 1929.

After the Second World War, during which enormous abuses of the principles of humanitarian law were witnessed, the existing provisions were extended and further codified. Legal protection for combatants and non-combatants consists of the rules that govern the conduct of military operations, known as the 'Law of the Hague', and the laws that protect victims of war, which are mainly set out in the four Geneva Conventions of 1949.[77] Almost all countries of the world became parties to these Conventions. Nowadays the distinction between 'Geneva law' and 'Hague law' is a rather artificial one, as the two 1977 Additional Protocols to the Geneva Conventions contain rules of both types.

The Additional Protocol I[78] relates to the protection of civilians and civilian property during international armed conflicts and the Additional Protocol II[79] relates to the protection of civilians and civilian property in national armed conflicts.

One of the main principles of international humanitarian law is the principle of proportionality. For example, no arms may be used that cause excessive and unnecessary suffering, or which cannot be sure of hitting a military target.

The Geneva Conventions prohibit without discrimination unlawful killing, torture, unfair trials and forced labour during international and national conflicts. The Conventions also require respect and protection of wounded, sick and shipwrecked members of armed forces, as well as prisoners of war, in times of international armed conflict. The Fourth Convention concerns the protection of civilians in time of war. The Additional Protocols extend the protection to all persons affected by armed conflict and forbid attacks on civilian populations and civilian objects by the combatants and parties to the conflict.[80]

The World Conference on Human Rights (1993) appealed to States that have not yet done so, to accede to the Geneva Conventions of 12 August 1949 and the Protocols thereto, and to take all appropriate national measures, including legislative ones, for their full implementation.

As a neutral intermediary in armed conflicts and disturbances, the International Committee of the Red Cross (ICRC)[81] attempts, either on its own initiative or basing its action on the Geneva Conventions and their Additional Protocols, to provide protection and assistance to the victims of international and national armed conflicts.

70. What are the functions of the ad hoc tribunals and court, established to deal with massive and gross violations of humanitarian law?

An international tribunal was established by Resolutions 808 and 827 (1993) of the United Nations Security Council for the prosecution of persons responsible for 'serious violations of international humanitarian law committed in the territory of the former Yugoslavia since 1991'. In accordance with its Statute, the International Criminal Tribunal for the former Yugoslavia (ICTY) is empowered to prosecute persons who are alleged to have committed

grave breaches of the Geneva Conventions of 1949 (Article 2); violations of the laws or customs of war (Article 3); genocide (Article 4) as defined by the Convention on the Prevention and Punishment of the Crime of Genocide (see also Question 25); and crimes against humanity (which includes a list of inhumane acts: murder, extermination, enslavement, deportation, imprisonment, torture, rape, prosecution on political, racial or religious grounds), when committed during international and national armed conflict and directed against any civilian population (Article 5). The ICTY, based in the Hague, the Netherlands, has the purpose of prosecuting and punishing persons responsible for such violations.

The ICTY consists of eleven independent judges and an independent Prosecutor, who is responsible for investigations and prosecutions. Proceedings may only be initiated by the Prosecutor. In conducting the investigations, the Prosecutor has the power to question suspects, victims and witnesses; to collect evidence; and to conduct on-site investigations. Information may be collected and received from any source. All Member States of the United Nations are obliged to cooperate fully with the ICTY, both in the preparation of cases, including the forwarding of information, the surrendering of accused persons and the implementation of the decisions. An accused person will enjoy all the guarantees of a fair trial. The penalty for a person found guilty of serious violations of international humanitarian law by the International Tribunal is imprisonment. The sentence will be carried out in the territory of a consenting State. The death penalty is not permitted under the Statute of the ICTY. Provision is made for an appeal process. The ICTY must submit an annual report on its activities to the Security Council and the General Assembly.[82]

The ICTY is a Tribunal established on an *ad hoc* basis, which means that it is not a permanent body and its work should be concluded at a certain point. According to the Tribunal's 'completion strategy' all first instance trials are to be completed by 2010 and appeals are to be concluded by the end of 2011. Since 2003 the Tribunal has worked closely with local judiciaries and courts in the countries of the former Yugoslavia, working in partnership as part of its effort to empower the local judiciary.

The Security Council, expressing its 'grave concern at the reports indicating that genocide and other systematic, widespread

and flagrant violations of international humanitarian law had been committed in Rwanda', adopted Resolution 955 (8 November 1994) setting up the ad hoc International Criminal Tribunal for Rwanda (ICTR). The jurisdiction of the Tribunal extends to persons responsible for such violations committed on the territory of Rwanda and Rwandan citizens responsible for genocide and other such violations committed on the territory of neighbouring States.

The proscribed acts include genocide (Article 2), crimes against humanity (Article 3) and violations of Common Article 3 of the Geneva Conventions and its additional Second Protocol. The temporal jurisdiction of the Tribunal is limited to acts committed between 1 January 1994 and 31 December 1994. The Tribunal consists of eleven judges and a prosecutor and is based in Arusha, Tanzania.

In accordance with Security Council Resolution 1503 (2003), the ICTR, like the ICTY, has a 'completion strategy'. According to it, the investigations should be completed by the end of 2004, all trial activities at first instance by the end of 2008, and all its work by the end of 2010.[83]

In June 2000, the Government of Sierra Leone requested the assistance of the United Nations for the establishment of a court to try people who, beginning on 30 November 1996, had taken part in committing atrocities during the civil war in Sierra Leone. The Statute for the Special Court for Sierra Leone[84] was signed by the United Nations and Sierra Leone on 16 January 2002. Following the incorporation of the Statute of the Special Court into the domestic law of Sierra Leone in the Special Court Agreement (Ratification) Act (Sierra Leone) on 7 March 2002, the Court was established and is now operative.

The Special Court for Sierra Leone differs from the international criminal tribunals above, in that it has jurisdiction to try crimes both under international and domestic law. The Court has concurrent jurisdiction with national courts and will try serious violations of international humanitarian law, as well as certain crimes committed under domestic law relating to the abuse of girls and the wanton destruction of property. However, the Court will only be able to try crimes under domestic law committed after 7 July 1999, pursuant to the Lome Peace Accord whereby an amnesty

was granted to all combatants, except for serious violations of humanitarian law. All persons who are brought before the Court will bear individual responsibility for their actions. The Special Court is composed of Trial Chambers and an Appeals Chamber, an Office of an Independent Prosecutor and a Registry. They are staffed by both Sierra Leonean and international personnel. As of 31 May 2009, two cases have been completed, including appeals and eleven people stand indicted by the Court.

71. What are the responsibilities of the International Criminal Court (ICC)?

On 17 July 1998 an international conference of 160 States in Rome adopted the Rome Statute of the International Criminal Court, which established the legal framework for the world's first permanent court dealing with gross violations of humanitarian law, crimes against humanity, genocide and the crime of aggression. Following upon ratification of the treaty by 60 States on 11 April 2002, the Court was established on 1 July 2002. It is based in the Hague (the Netherlands).

The ICC is entitled to consider cases brought against individuals, aged 18 and above, accused of committing the most serious crimes: genocide, crimes against humanity, war crimes and aggression. The first three of these crimes are clearly defined by the Statute. The definition of the crime of aggression remains to be agreed upon by the Assembly of States Parties before the Court can consider such cases.[85]'Genocide' covers specifically listed acts committed with the intention of destroying, in whole or in part, a national, religious, ethnic or racial group. 'Crimes against humanity' covers specifically prohibited acts (e.g. murder, extermination, rape, sexual slavery, and torture) committed as part of a widespread or systematic attack directed against any civilian population. 'War crimes' covers grave breaches of the 1949 Geneva Conventions and other serious violations of the laws of war, committed on a large scale during international and internal armed conflicts. The maximum sentence the Court can impose for these crimes is thirty years in prison, and it can also decide upon compensation to the victims.

Cases can be brought before the ICC for investigation or trial if they have been referred to the independent Prosecutor by a State Party, if the Prosecutor has initiated an investigation with the authorization of the Pre-Trial Chamber, or if they have been referred by the Security Council of the United Nations in accordance with Chapter VII of the UN Charter. The Court has jurisdiction in cases where the suspect is a national of States that have ratified or acceded to the treaty or when the act is committed on their territory. States not party to the treaty can accept the Court's jurisdiction on an *ad hoc* basis. The jurisdiction of the Court is limited to crimes committed after the Statute came into force (1 July 2002), and the Court has no powers to deal with violations committed before that date. Further, the Court can only investigate or try cases where the State is unwilling or unable to do this itself. In cases where a State has provided a free and fair investigation or trial the Court has no jurisdiction with regard to the case, whatever the outcome.

The Court is composed of a Presidency, Chambers (Appeals, Trial and Pre-Trial), the Office of the Prosecutor and the Registry. The Court has eighteen judges, serving a maximum of nine years, who are divided into the three Chambers depending on their expertise. Three of the judges are elected to the Presidency (a President and First and Second Vice-President) and are responsible for the proper judicial administration of the Court. This does not include the Office of the Prosecutor, which is to remain independent. The Court is accountable to the Assembly of States Parties. The States Parties oversee the Court's work and provide management oversight regarding its administration for the President, the Prosecutor and the Registrar; decide on budgetary matters; decide whether to change the number of judges; and consider any questions relating to the lack of cooperation of a State with the Court.

As of 31 May 2009, the Court has initiated proceedings of four cases and has issued twelve arrest warrants.[86] The Court's first trial began on 26 January 2009.

United Nations bodies, programmes and specialized agencies dealing with human rights

72. What is the role of the United Nations High Commissioner for Human Rights?

Following upon a recommendation of the Vienna Declaration and Programme of Action (1993)[87] the United Nations General Assembly unanimously adopted Resolution 48/141 of 20 December 1993 establishing the post of the High Commissioner for Human Rights. The first High Commissioner took up duties on 5 April 1994. The High Commissioner is the principal United Nations official with responsibility for human rights and is accountable to the Secretary-General of the United Nations.

The High Commissioner, appointed for four years with the possibility of one term renewal, must function within the framework of the United Nations Charter, the Universal Declaration of

Human Rights and other relevant instruments to promote universal respect for and observance of all human rights. In addition, he or she must be guided by the recognition that all human rights – civil, cultural, economic, political and social – are universal, indivisible, interdependent and interrelated, and that the promotion and protection of human rights is the legitimate concern of the international community.

The responsibilities of the High Commissioner are: to protect and promote the effective enjoyment by all of all human rights; to co-ordinate human rights promotion and protection throughout the United Nations system; and to advise the Secretary-General on United Nations policies in the area of human rights. In carrying out his/her task, the High Commissioner engages in dialogue with all governments and seeks the promotion and protection of human rights.

Responsibilities in specific fields include: the promotion and protection of the right to development, the coordination of relevant United Nations education and public information programmes in the field of human rights; and the rationalization, adaptation, strengthening and streamlining of the United Nations machinery in the field of human rights with a view to improving its efficiency and its effectiveness. The High Commissioner is responsible for carrying out overall supervision of the Office of the High Commissioner for Human Rights (OHCHR), through which advisory services and technical and financial assistance are provided in support of actions and programmes in the field of human rights.

73. What is the mission of the Office of the High Commissioner for Human Rights (OHCHR)?

The core mission of OHCHR is to 'work for the protection of all human rights for all people; to help empower people to realize their rights; and to assist those responsible for upholding such rights in ensuring that they are implemented'.[88]

The OHCHR serves as a focal point for United Nations activities in the field of human rights. The Office thus supports the United Nations human rights system, which consists broadly

of the Human Rights Council and its mechanisms (including the Universal Periodic Review Mechanism), the Human Rights Trust Fund and the treaty body system. The latter comprises eight human rights bodies that monitor the implementation at the national level of the following instruments: International Covenant on Economic, Social and Cultural Rights (ICESCR); International Covenant on Civil and Political Rights (ICCPR); International Covenant on the Elimination of Racial Discrimination (ICERD); Convention on the Elimination of All Forms of Discrimination against Women (CEDAW); Convention on the Rights of the Child (CRC); Convention Against Torture (CAT); Convention on the Protection of the Rights of all Migrant Workers and Members of their Families (see Question 52) and the Convention on the Rights of Persons with Disabilities (see Question 53).[89]

It also services the four human rights trust funds that provide assistance to victims of torture, support for work on contemporary forms of slavery as well as assistance for the rights of indigenous peoples.[90]

The wide range of activities carried out by the OHCHR also includes: assisting in the creation of independent national human rights institutions; spearheading a global campaign towards combating racism, xenophobia and related intolerance (see Questions 34–35); ongoing support for the Permanent Forum on Indigenous Issues (see Question 51); assistance to various regions in identifying their specific human rights needs and strategies to address them, i.e. human rights support for the New Partnership for Africa's Development (NEPAD); assisting States towards ratification of international human rights instruments and the follow-up and implementation of these; and assisting societies in conflict. In addition, OHCHR attempts to integrate a gender perspective into all of its activities and mainstream human rights in all the United Nations' activities and functions.

The OHCHR carries out research and studies on human rights and prepares reports on their implementation. It also coordinates liaison with non-governmental and other organizations active in the field of human rights, as well as with the media. Furthermore, it disseminates information and prepares publications related to human rights and promotes human rights education worldwide. The OHCHR held the responsibility of coordinating the activities

within the framework of the United Nations Decade for Human Rights Education (1995–2004) (see Questions 108–110).

A number of resolutions of the United Nations General Assembly have stressed the importance of the activities of the Office and the necessity to ensure adequate human, financial and other resources for its work. Only part of OHCHR funds derive from the UN regular budget ($119.2 million for 2008-2009). Voluntary contributions, for which OHCHR appeals to States, constitute an important part of its budget (US$ 95.7 million in 2007). In the 2005 World Summit, the UN Member States made a commitment to double the OHCHR's share in the UN regular budget within five years.

74. What is the purpose of the Technical Cooperation Programme of the OHCHR?

The most practical work that OHCHR undertakes to promote and protect human rights is through its extensive technical cooperation programme. This programme supports States' own efforts to build national protection systems. Based on an assessment of domestic needs, an integrated technical assistance programme is elaborated with the aim of strengthening a legal and institutional framework that can promote and sustain human rights and democracy under the rule of law. The OHCHR also works with other United Nations agencies and with regional human rights organizations. It has established regional representatives in different regions to assist with its technical cooperation work.

Within this context, assistance is provided for incorporating human rights standards into national laws, policies and practices and building sustainable national capacities to implement these standards. This assistance is also provided at the regional level. Support activities include providing advice on mechanisms to secure democratic order, such as electoral assistance and the training of judges, law-enforcement personnel, public officials and the armed forces, with particular reference to international human rights standards.

The programme also has the following components: human rights education, strengthening the role of the mass media in the promotion of human rights, and human rights activities in support

of peacemaking, peacekeeping and peacebuilding. The latter focuses on conflict prevention and techniques for peaceful resolutions. This includes the training of United Nations peacekeepers with protection mandates and the establishment of field offices.[91]

The programme recognizes the crucial role of non-governmental human rights organizations and other community groups in building civil society, and provides direct support for their projects. The 2005 World Summit underlined the importance of the work of the OHCHR and its contribution in the areas of technical assistance and capacity-building, according to the OHCHR's Plan of Action.[92]

75. What is the contribution of UNESCO to the promotion and protection of human rights and fundamental freedoms?

UNESCO (the United Nations Educational, Scientific and Cultural Organization) was created in 1945. It is a specialized agency of the United Nations system with 193 Member States and 6 Associate members. The organization's governing bodies are its General Conference and the Executive Board.

In accordance with its Constitution, UNESCO should 'contribute to peace and security by promoting collaboration among nations through education, science and culture in order to further universal respect for justice, for the rule of law and for the human rights and fundamental freedoms which are affirmed for the peoples of the world, without distinction of race, sex, language or religion, by the Charter of the United Nations'.

UNESCO has special responsibility with regard to certain rights, in particular: the right to education; the right to participate in cultural life; the right to freedom of opinion and expression, including the right to seek, receive and impart information; and the right to enjoy the benefits of scientific progress and its applications. UNESCO's action to promote human rights includes standard-setting activities, conducting research and disseminating knowledge on human rights (see Question 108).

The 1960 Convention Against Discrimination in Education provides for the elimination and prevention of any form of dis-

crimination in education (Article 3), as well as for the adoption of measures that promote equality of opportunity and treatment (Article 4). The 2005 World Summit recognized the importance of the 'UNESCO strategy for the eradication of poverty, especially extreme poverty, in supporting the Education for All programmes as a tool to achieve the millennium development goal of universal primary education by 2015'.[93] The fight against racism and racial discrimination has always been a priority for the Organization. Through research, education and the media, UNESCO has worked since its creation to demonstrate the fallacious nature of theories of racial superiority and to promote a spirit of tolerance and dialogue among civilizations. These efforts were paralleled by the adoption of standard-setting instruments, such as the Declaration on Race and Racial Prejudice (1978) and the Declaration of Principles on Tolerance (1995). Since the 2001 World Conference against Racism, in Durban, South Africa, UNESCO has given particular attention to the fight against racism at the municipal level. Hence, it launched the creation in 2004 of an International Coalition of Cities against Racism. UNESCO's efforts to mobilize local authorities against racism and develop an integrated strategy to combat racism, racial discrimination, xenophobia and related intolerance were acknowledged and encouraged by the Durban Review Conference, as referred to in its Outcome Document (Outcome Document of the Durban Review Conference, par. 142, see Question 35).

UNESCO has also undertaken numerous activities in order to further develop the right to participate in cultural life and to promote cultural diversity. The Declaration of the Principles of International Cultural Cooperation (1966) stresses that 'each culture has a dignity and value which must be respected and preserved' and that 'every people has the right and the duty to develop its culture' (Article 1). The Recommendation on Participation by the People at Large in Cultural Life and Their Contribution to It (1976) defines access to culture as opportunities available for everyone for obtaining information, training and knowledge, and for enjoying cultural values, in particular through the creation of appropriate socio-economic conditions.

In 2001, the UNESCO General Conference adopted the Universal Declaration on Cultural Diversity. Affirming that cultural diversity is the common heritage of humankind, the Declaration

calls for respect for cultural diversity as one of the roots of development and a determining factor for international peace and stability. Moreover, it emphasizes that the full implementation of all human rights, and cultural rights in particular, is a prerequisite for the promotion of cultural diversity. The Convention on the Protection and Promotion of the Diversity of Cultural Expressions was adopted in 2005 (see Question 76).

A number of instruments protecting the rights of persons playing an important role in cultural and scientific life have been adopted.[94] In particular, since 1989, UNESCO has been engaged in encouraging and assisting Member States in designing and adapting their media, information and communication laws in accordance with human rights principles and internationally recognized democratic standards.

An important part of UNESCO's work in the fields of social and human sciences is the conduct of inter-disciplinary research to study the social, economic and cultural changes resulting from the ongoing process of globalization and the current model of development. Issues such as migration and the rights of migrants, poverty reduction and human rights have been the subject of research activities and operational projects.

Responding to the challenges emerging from progress in research on human genetic data, UNESCO adopted the Universal Declaration on Human Genome and Human Rights (1997). The Declaration strikes a balance between safeguarding respect for human rights and fundamental freedoms and the need to ensure

THEY MAY NOT BE THE FIRST IN THEIR CLASS, BUT IN CIVICS, THEY'RE THE BEST!

freedom of research. It states that research and treatment shall be carried out in full respect of human dignity and that no one shall be the subject of discrimination on the basis of genetic character-istics. The 2005 Universal Declaration on Bioethics and Human Rights was a response to a wide range of complex ethical dilemmas raised by the developments in the areas of medicine and various life sciences. The Declaration establishes universally agreed ethical guidelines drawing upon the principles of human rights. In doing so, it clearly recognizes the interrelation between ethics and human rights in the specific field of bioethics.

76. What monitoring mechanism exists within UNESCO?

The procedures whereby UNESCO can take action, regarding the promotion and implementation of human rights, are partly provided for by the conventions and recommendations it has adopted. The method used is a reporting and complaints system.

The UNESCO Convention against Discrimination in Education entered into force in 1962 and, as of 31 May 2009, ninety-five States have become parties to it.[95] This Convention commits States Parties to a national policy that will promote equal-ity of opportunity and treatment in matters of education. States Parties undertake to ensure, by legislation if required, that there is no discrimination in the admission of pupils to educational institu-tions, nor any discrimination in the treatment of students. Foreign nationals are assured the same access to education. The measures for implementation are based on a system of reports from the participating States, which are examined by a special Committee on Conventions and Recommendations. The report and comments of the Committee are then submitted to the General Conference of UNESCO. The only further action taken is in the form of resolutions passed by the General Conference on the basis of the issues raised.

To supplement and strengthen this system, a Conciliation and Good Office Commission was created under a Protocol to the Convention[96] to deal with complaints from States alleging that another State Party is not giving effect to the provisions of the

Convention. The Commission's mandate is to seek an amicable solution or, failing this, to make a recommendation that could include a request to the International Court of Justice for an opinion (the latter procedure, however, has never been applied).

Other procedures exist for the implementation of other UNESCO instruments relating to such matters as the status of teachers. The joint International Labour Organization/UNESCO Committee of Experts on the Application of the Recommendation concerning the Status of Teachers (1966) was set up in 1968 by a decision of UNESCO's Executive Board and by the Governing Body of the ILO. The Committee is made up of twelve independent experts, half of whom are chosen by the ILO and the other half by UNESCO. Discussions are under way on the desirability of updating the Recommendation and including some of the aspects covered by it in a possible convention on the status of teachers. In keeping with the fact that this body now monitors the application of both normative instruments, the Executive Board decided[97] that the name of the Joint Committee be changed to the 'Joint ILO/UNESCO Committee of Experts on the Application of the Recommendations concerning Teaching Personnel' (CEART), as suggested by the Joint Committee, in order better to reflect the Committee's expanded mandate as decided.[98]

UNESCO has also undertaken efforts to protect cultural property, considering that this field of interest is closely linked with cultural rights. There are three UNESCO Conventions that address the issue of cultural property: the Convention for the Protection of Cultural Property in the Event of Armed Conflict (the 'Hague' Convention), with Regulations for the Execution of the Convention, as well as the Protocol to the Convention and the Conference Resolutions (1954); the Convention on the Means of Prohibiting and Preventing the Illicit Import, Export and Transfer of Ownership of Cultural Property (1970); and the Convention concerning the Protection of the World Cultural and Natural Heritage (1972).

In October 2005, the General Conference of UNESCO adopted the Convention on the Protection and Promotion of the Diversity of Cultural Expressions. This standard-setting instrument identifies a series of rights and obligations of the States Parties for the promotion and protection of the diversity of cultural expres-

sions. It establishes two organs: the Conference of Parties, which is the plenary and supreme body of the Convention, and the Intergovernmental Committee[99], which has the responsibility for the promotion of the objectives of the Convention and for encouraging and monitoring its implementation. The Convention entered into force on 18 March 2007 and has been ratified, as of 31 May 2009, by 98 States and the European Community.[100]

The question of improving the effectiveness of these mechanisms was examined at several sessions of the Executive Board. The Executive Board and ECOSOC established in October 2001 a Joint Expert Group on monitoring the right to education. The Group was mandated to examine possibilities for reducing the reporting burden in States and for increasing the effectiveness of existing procedures. The General Conference at its 32nd session in October 2003 called for a thematic organization of State reports relating to conventions and recommendations and that information gathered by the treaty bodies of the UN be taken into account.

77. Can UNESCO receive complaints of alleged violations of human rights?

UNESCO has a procedure for handling complaints from alleged victims or any person, group of persons, or national or international non-governmental organization having reliable knowledge of an alleged violation of human rights in the Organization's fields of competence, namely, education, science, culture and communication. If and when consent is given by complainants for their names to be divulged, the government concerned is informed and asked to submit any written comments it may have regarding the complaints. These comments are referred to as 'communications'. The communications, together with relevant replies, if any, from governments, are examined in camera by the Executive Board's Committee on Conventions and Recommendations. Representatives of governments concerned may attend meetings of the Committee in order to provide additional information or answer questions from members of the Committee. The Committee first examines the admissibility of each communication and then, if the communication is declared admissible and considered to warrant

further action, it seeks to help bring about a friendly solution designed to advance the promotion of human rights falling within UNESCO's fields of competence. The Committee's next step is to submit a confidential report to the Executive Board of UNESCO, which may take whatever action it considers appropriate.

This procedure not only concerns individual and specific cases of violations of human rights, but also 'questions' of massive, systematic or flagrant violations. A question is considered to exist when there is either an accumulation of individual cases forming a consistent pattern of gross violations of human rights or a policy contrary to human rights applied *de jure* or *de facto* by a State. Communications relating to questions of violations of human rights may be considered at public meetings of the Executive Board or of the General Conference. To date, this procedure has not been used.

The UNESCO procedures are subject, in some respects, to less stringent preconditions than some of the other international and regional procedures for dealing with alleged violations of human rights. For example, they do not require that all domestic remedies be exhausted, but only proof that an attempt has been made to exhaust those remedies. Also the fact that a case is being examined by another international organization does not prevent it from being considered under UNESCO procedures.

From 1978 to 2007, 545 communications were considered by the Committee on Conventions and Recommendations, of which 344 were satisfactorily resolved, mainly through dialogue between the Committee and the States concerned. The reports and cases examined by the Committee are confidential, but according to the 2005 Rules of Procedure of the Executive Board (based on Rule 29), the Board's private documents are normally made accessible to the public after a period of twenty years.[101]

78. What is the contribution of the International Labour Organization (ILO) to the promotion and protection of human rights and fundamental freedoms?

The ILO, which has been in existence since 1919 and became a specialized agency of the United Nations system in 1946, seeks to achieve social justice through its activities in the social and labour fields. This goal is known as the achievement of 'Decent Work'. The basis of ILO action for human rights is the establishment of international labour standards and the supervision of the implementation of these standards by Member States of the organization, and technical assistance to States and others to put these standards and principles into effect.[102]

The ILO is a tripartite organization, which means that all policy-making bodies of the organization are composed of representatives of governments, employers and workers, who participate on an equal footing in the decision-making and monitoring procedures of the organization.

International labour standards are adopted by the main body of the ILO, the International Labour Conference, in the form of conventions or recommendations. The conventions relate to the basic human rights within the fields of competence of the ILO, such as freedom of association, abolition of forced labour, freedom from discrimination in employment and occupation, child labour, etc. They also lay down standards in such fields as conditions of work, occupational safety and health, social security, industrial relations, employment policy and vocational guidance, and provide for the protection of special groups, such as women, migrants and indigenous and tribal peoples.

79. What are the monitoring procedures within the ILO?

There are various procedures for supervising and monitoring the implementation of ILO standards. When States ratify conventions, they also undertake to submit periodic reports on the measures they have taken to give effect to the provisions of the convention.

These reports must always be sent by governments to the workers' and employers' organizations in each country, which may submit comments. An independent twenty-member Committee of Experts on the Application of Conventions and Recommendations examines the reports and comments on the degree of compliance by governments. In its assessment, the Committee allows a certain flexibility in implementing a convention, but differences in political, economic or social systems do not modify governments' obligations, especially in regard to fundamental human rights. The Committee submits a report to the annual International Labour Conference, which is examined by the Conference Committee on the Application of Conventions and Recommendations. This Committee is a tripartite body, composed of representatives of governments, workers and employers. Over the years, the ILO standard-setting and supervisory activities have had a considerable influence on changing the social and labour legislation of Member States and have helped to improve the conditions and lives of working people.

Where there are difficulties in complying with conventions, the ILO offers assistance to the countries concerned to help find solutions. This is done through a network of technical advisers throughout the world, and by a variety of other means. ILO technical assistance in all fields is based on its standards. Moreover, States are required to report on the obstacles to ratification of ILO conventions.

80. Can the ILO receive complaints of alleged violations of human rights?

Apart from the regular supervisory function of the ILO, based on reports from governments, there are two complaints procedures under the ILO Constitution for the implementation of labour standards. The first allows any employers' or workers' organization to make a representation to the ILO claiming that a Member State has failed to comply with its obligations in respect of a convention it has ratified. A special tripartite committee of the Governing Body of the ILO examines the case to determine whether the convention is in fact being applied.

The second procedure allows a Member State to make a complaint against another Member State if it considers that the latter is not ensuring effective observance of any convention that they have both ratified. A complaint may also be made by the Governing Body, either on its own initiative or on receipt of a complaint from a delegate to the annual International Labour Conference. The Governing Body may appoint a commission of inquiry. If the government in question does not accept the findings of the commission, it may refer the case to the International Court of Justice. This has not yet happened, as the findings of the commissions of inquiry have generally been accepted by the governments concerned. Recently the ILO has also invoked an article of its Constitution that allows it to take other measures to ensure that a complaint is properly followed, soliciting the assistance of other international organizations as well as governments worldwide. Only a relatively limited number of representations and complaints have been made, but they have related to important questions, particularly linked with trade union rights, discrimination and forced labour.

81. What ILO procedure exists to safeguard trade union rights?

In 1950, the ILO established a special procedure for examining allegations of violations of trade union rights and also the rights of employers' organizations, which supplements the general supervisory procedures for conventions. Complaints may be submitted by workers' or employers' organizations, or by governments. In practice, most complaints are made by national or international trade unions and complaints may relate to all trade union rights, including those not covered by the two principal conventions: the Convention (No. 87) concerning Freedom of Association and Protection of the Right to Organize (1948) and the Convention (No. 98) concerning the Application of Principles of the Rights to Organize and to Bargain Collectively (1949). Complaints may be made against any government, whether it has ratified the conventions or not. The tripartite Committee on Freedom of Association of the Governing Body examines these allegations and may refer complaints for further

investigation to a Fact-Finding and Conciliation Commission on Freedom of Association. In practice, the Committee itself has examined almost all the complaints received. The recommendations of the Committee have prompted action, ranging from the repeal or amendment of legislation and the reinstatement of dismissed workers to the release of imprisoned trade unionists. In some cases, death sentences of trade unionists have been commuted. Between 1952 and 2008 the Committee received and examined more than 2000 complaints.

82. What standards has the ILO adopted concerning the effect of globalization on the protection of labour rights?

In June 1998, the ILO adopted the Declaration on Fundamental Principles and Rights at Work and its follow-up. The Declaration recognizes the new challenges brought about by the process of globalization and trade liberalization to the struggle for workers' rights. The breakdown of trade barriers often leads to a lowering of domestic standards by governments, as a means of ensuring the greater competitiveness of domestic business and industry. This has necessitated the reaffirmation of social policies, and the Declaration aims at ensuring that social progress goes hand in hand with economic development. To this end the Declaration reaffirms the commitment of the international community and of all ILO Member States to 'respect, to promote and to realise in good faith' four principles recognized in the eight fundamental ILO Conventions. These are: the right of workers and employers to freedom of association and the effective recognition of the right to collective bargaining (Conventions Nos. 87 and 98); the elimination of all forms of forced or compulsory labour (Nos. 29 and 105); the effective abolition of child labour (Nos. 138 and 182); and the elimination of discrimination in respect of employment and occupation (Nos. 100 and 111). The Declaration prohibits the use of labour standards for protectionist trade purposes and affirms that the comparative advantage of any country in the production of goods and services should not be affected by the Declaration and its follow-up.

States are obliged to protect these principles in their domestic legislation and in practice. However, the Declaration also recognizes the obligation of the ILO to assist Member States in reaching these objectives by making full use of its constitutional, operational and budgetary resources to promote the fundamental Conventions and to create a climate for economic and social development.

The Declaration sets out a Promotional Follow-up towards implementing these objectives, which focuses on two promotional reporting tools of the ILO: the Annual Review and the Global Report. There is also a large programme of technical assistance for the implementation of these rights, supplementing the already existing International Programme for the Elimination of Child Labour (IPEC).

The Annual Review is composed of reports from governments describing the efforts made to respect the principles and rights relating to all unratified, fundamental ILO Conventions, and comments from workers' and employers' organizations. These

reports provide a baseline against which countries can measure their own progress. The Global Report, submitted each year by the ILO Director-General to the International Labour Conference, considers the situation with regard to one of the categories of principles and rights. In a four-year period, all four principles and rights are reviewed. The report serves as a basis for determining future priorities, so that the ILO, through its technical cooperation activities, can assist its members in implementing the Fundamental Principles and Rights. In the outcome document of the World Summit for Social Development of July 2000, States committed themselves to improving the quality of work in the context of globalization, including through promotion of these and other ILO initiatives. The ILO is also participating in a number of other initiatives that are closely based on its standards and principles, such as the UN's Global Compact (four of the nine principles reflect labour rights), and the Poverty Reduction Strategy Papers approach.

83. What other initiatives has the ILO taken towards addressing the social dimension of globalization?

The ILO has launched a World Commission on the Social Dimension of Globalization to consider the social consequences of globalization. This Commission, which held its first meeting in March 2002, was led by two Heads of State and its membership was drawn from all regions of the world. Its ultimate goal was to find ways whereby the process of globalization could contribute to the reduction of poverty and unemployment, and to the fostering of growth and sustainable development. It aimed to formulate concrete actions to guide and shape the process of globalization towards promoting fair sharing of its benefits. In 2004 the Commission delivered its Final Report, called 'A Fair Globalization: Creating Opportunities for All'. In this Report, the Commission proposed a strategy for the change of the effects of globalization through a series of recommendations.[103]

An important step forward was the adoption, on 10 June 2008, at the 97th Session of the International Labour Conference, of

the ILO Declaration on Social Justice for a Fair Globalization. The Declaration expresses the contemporary vision of the ILO's mandate in the era of globalization. In this document, the representatives of governments and of employers' and workers' organizations from 182 Member States emphasized the key role of the Organization in helping to achieve progress and social justice in the context of globalization. They committed themselves to enhancing the ILO's capacity to advance these goals, through the Decent Work Agenda.[104] The Declaration institutionalizes the Decent Work concept developed by the ILO since 1999, placing it at the core of the Organization's policies.

84. What is the contribution of the Food and Agriculture Organization (FAO) to the promotion and protection of human rights and fundamental freedoms?

The Food and Agriculture Organization (FAO) is the largest specialized agency of the United Nations system. It was founded in 1945 with a mandate to raise levels of nutrition, to improve agricultural productivity and to better the conditions of the rural population. The FAO seeks to alleviate poverty and hunger by promoting agricultural development, improved nutrition and food security. The ultimate goal is to meet the needs of both present and future generations by promoting development that does not degrade the environment and is technically appropriate, economically viable and socially acceptable. The governing body of the FAO is the Conference of Member States, which meets every two years to review the work carried out by the Organization and approve a Programme of Work and Budget for the next biennium. The role of FAO in the field of human rights is mainly based on the World Food Summit organized in 1996. In accordance with objective 7.4 of the Plan of Action of that Summit, FAO's strategic framework for 2000–2015 includes an approach to food security based on human rights. Furthermore, in 2002, FAO hosted the 'World Food Summit: Five Years Later' which adopted a declaration 'reaffirming the right of everyone to have access to safe and nutritious food'.

85. What is the contribution of the World Health Organization (WHO) to the promotion and protection of human rights and fundamental freedoms?

The World Health Organization (WHO), the United Nations specialized agency for health, was established on 7 April 1948. WHO's objective is the attainment by all peoples of the highest possible level of health. In its Constitution, health is affirmed as a fundamental human right, which was reaffirmed in its World Health Declaration, adopted in 1998. The governing body of WHO is the World Health Assembly, composed of representatives of the 193 Member States. The main tasks of the World Health Assembly are to approve the WHO programme and budget for each biennium and to decide upon major policy questions. WHO acts as the directing and coordinating authority on international health activities. The organization transmits policy decisions on international health matters, promotes international agreements on health policies, encourages the rationalization and mobilization of resources for health and supports developing countries by identifying their needs for external resources. The World Health Assembly has adopted various regulations designed to prevent the international spread of disease and several resolutions on subjects related to the realization of rights provided in the International Covenants on Human Rights, such as nutrition, family health and medical research. A number of research and training activities have been organized on health and human rights, including the training of staff as well as the preparation of an annotated bibliography, a database of institutions, and guidelines on a human rights approach to tuberculosis. The World Health Report is issued by the WHO annually. The 2008 issue focused on the need to promote primary health care.

86. What is the contribution of the United Nations Children's Fund (UNICEF) to the promotion and protection of human rights and fundamental freedoms?

The United Nations Children's Fund (UNICEF) is mandated to advocate the protection of children's rights, to help meet their basic needs and to expand their opportunities to reach their full potential.

UNICEF is guided by the provisions and principles of the Convention on the Rights of the Child and its two optional Protocols. As UNICEF is also mandated to promote the equal rights of women and girls, the Convention on the Elimination of All Forms of Discrimination against Women is central to the work of the organization. Other international human rights standards guiding the practical work of UNICEF are ILO Conventions 138 and 182 and the Hague Convention on Inter-Country Adoption. UNICEF offices work with national partners to identify rights-based approaches to complex problems affecting the realization of human rights such as: maternal mortality, HIV/AIDS, child labour, malnutrition, violence against children and the access of girls to education. With the aim of contributing to a 'World Fit for Children', UNICEF emphasizes the inseparable connection between the promotion of children's and women's rights and the progressive and sustained achievement of human development goals.

87. What is the contribution of the United Nations Development Programme (UNDP) to the promotion and protection of human rights and fundamental freedoms?

The UNDP was founded in 1965 and aims to promote technical and economic advancement in developing countries. The organization advocates the protection of human rights in the fields of democratic governance, poverty reduction, crisis prevention and recovery, energy and environment, information and communications technology, and HIV/AIDS. UNDP works with 174 governments through a network of 146 country offices and other programmes worldwide.

Its major programmes and policy decisions are determined by a 36-member Executive Board composed of representatives of both developed and developing countries. The main focus of UNDP is helping countries and sharing solutions by establishing a global network and, through this type of coordination, ensuring the most effective use of United Nations and international aid resources. Every year since 1990, UNDP launches the Human Development Report. Its aim is to put people at the centre of the development process in terms of economic debate, policy and advocacy, and to go beyond income to assess the level of people's long-term well-being. Since the first Report, four new composite indices for human development have been developed – the Human Development Index, the Gender-related Development Index, the Gender Empowerment Measure, and the Human Poverty Index. Each Report also focuses on a specific theme in the current development debate, providing path-breaking analysis and policy recommendations.

The Reports' messages – and the tools to implement them – have been embraced by people around the world, as evidenced by the publication of national human development reports at the country level in more than 140 nations. The Human Development Report is an independent report. It is the product of a selected team of leading scholars, development practitioners and members of the Human Development Report Office of UNDP. The Report is translated into more than a dozen languages and made available in more than 100 countries annually.

88. How do the activities of the World Bank, the International Monetary Fund (IMF) and the World Trade Organization (WTO) relate to human rights?

Both the IMF and World Bank have been challenged for not developing a coherent human rights policy and agenda for their work. The World Bank has become more explicit, in recent years, in defining its lending policy in relation to human rights and allied issues, such as alleviation of poverty.

Recently, the World Bank has focused on food security by establishing a Global Food Crisis Response Programme, in

order to address problems linked with the global food crisis. This Programme is a part of the World Bank Group's New Deal on Global Food Policy, which has been endorsed by 150 countries. As of February 2009, $497 million was distributed in 30 countries, from a total budget of $866 million for this purpose. The Bank has also participated in the High Level Meeting on Food Security (Madrid, Spain, January 2009).

There is still debate on how appropriate it is for the Bank to act as a political or ethical reformer, how far it can go in terms of its legal mandate in addressing human rights considerations rather than purely economic ones and how coherent its involvement in human rights issues is. There are similar debates in relation to the IMF. In the case of the IMF, however, its policies of conditionality (which require cutting back on government and public sector spending) continue to arouse controversy. Many sectors of civil society have argued that these policies have led to a reduction in spending on critical social issues, such as education and health, and made the position of the rural poor, in particular, more precarious.

The WTO has been at the centre of a number of deeply contested debates involving human rights and development. A major debate involving the WTO has focused on the inclusion of a social clause, incorporating human rights and labour standards, within the General Agreement on Tariffs and Trade in 1994. At the Doha Ministerial Conference and at the previous Ministerial Conference held in Singapore, Ministers reaffirmed that the International Labour Organization is the competent body to deal with internationally recognized, core labour standards. At the heart of this debate is the issue of trade restrictions and whether or not they should be imposed on goods made in violation of core labour and human rights standards. Views on this issue differ widely. The debate continues to be an active one, with the focus shifting from incorporation of an explicit clause to reinterpretation of the agreement so as to include human rights and labour standards considerations within the WTO dispute settlement system.

Also subject to debate are the problems faced by developing countries in implementing their obligations under the WTO agreements, particularly in relation to agriculture (food security) and intellectual property (access to medicines, biodiversity). At the Ministerial Conference in Doha, Ministers agreed to adopt fifty

decisions, clarifying the obligations of developing countries with respect to a number of issues, and a future work programme for addressing a number of other concerns that were not settled at the Conference. Following the meeting in Doha, subsequent ministerial meetings took place in Cancún (2003) and Hong Kong (2005). Related negotiations took place in Geneva (2004, 2006, 2008); Paris (2005); and Potsdam (2007). As of May 2009, the Round had not been concluded.

Regional human rights instruments and procedures

89. How does the Council of Europe protect civil and political rights?

The Council of Europe, created in 1949 and based in Strasbourg, established a machinery for the protection of human rights in 1950, under the European Convention for the Protection of Human Rights and Fundamental Freedoms (also known as the European Convention on Human Rights). The Convention came into force on 3 September 1953. The Convention deals mainly with civil and political rights and states in the Preamble that the governments of European countries are resolved 'to take the first step for the collective enforcement of certain of the rights stated in the Universal Declaration of Human Rights'. The States Parties guarantee basic civil and political rights not only to their own citizens, but to all persons 'within their jurisdiction'.

Membership of the Council of Europe has grown to forty-seven States.[105] It is compulsory for all Council of Europe Member States to ratify the Convention and accept the right of individual petition and the jurisdiction of the European Court of Human Rights. The Convention is elaborated by 14 Protocols on substantive or practical issues regarding the functioning of the Court.

The machinery for guaranteeing enforcement of the rights protected under the European Convention currently consists of the European Court of Human Rights. The Committee of Ministers of the Council of Europe supervises the execution of the Court's judgements. The competence of these institutions extends to both inter-State cases and individual applications, which includes those from groups of individuals or NGOs.

The decisions of the Court are legally binding and States Parties are therefore obliged to comply with its findings. This commonly leads to States making legislative or other changes of a general character (usually to prevent the repetition of the violation) in response to the Court's judgements on specific cases. Examples include the following: Austria, Germany and Turkey have amended their laws on detention before trial; the United Kingdom has changed prison rules in order to comply with a judgement regarding the right of access to a court; the Netherlands has introduced amendments to its law on military discipline; Bulgaria has made an important reform in its criminal procedure; and France has changed the disciplinary procedures of certain professional bodies, making the proceedings public. In addition, the Court often requires States to pay costs and compensation to the person or persons whose rights have been violated. During 2008, the Court issued 1545 Judgements, in which violations of the Convention were found in 1543 cases. The Convention's Protocol No. 14, which is intended to guarantee the Court's long-term effectiveness, will enter into force once all the States Parties to the Convention have ratified it.[106]

The Council of Europe offers an extensive programme of practical assistance in the field of human rights, which aims at strengthening the transition towards democracy in new Member States, and at facilitating their integration into the Council of Europe.

90. How does the Council of Europe protect economic, social and cultural rights?

These rights are recognized by the European Social Charter (1961), which was revised in 1996. The revised European Social Charter came into force in 1999. Contracting parties[107] agreed to guarantee

rights to housing, health, education, employment, social protection and freedom of movement without any discrimination on grounds of race, sex, age, colour, language, religion, opinions, national origin, social background, state of health or association with a national minority. The Charter also establishes the European Committee of Social Rights, which monitors the implementation of the Charter. Each contracting party must submit a report to the Committee every year, indicating how they implement the Charter in law and practice. The Committee examines the reports and publishes 'conclusions' every year on the performance of Member States.

Under a protocol that came into force in 1998, collective complaints of violations of the Charter can be submitted to the European Committee of Social Rights. Collective complaints can be lodged by the European Workers' and Employers' Organisations; European Trade Union Confederation (ETUC); Union of Industrial and Employers' Confederations of Europe (UNICE); International Organisation of Employers (IOE); and European non-governmental organizations having consultative status with the Council of Europe and national employers' organizations, trade unions and national non-governmental organizations, if the State concerned has made a declaration authorizing them to do so. If a State takes no action on a decision of the European Committee on Social Rights, the Committee of Ministers may address a recommendation to that State, asking it to change the situation in law and in practice.

The aim of the collective complaints procedure is to increase participation from workers, employers and non-governmental organizations. It is also an example of a number of measures drawn up to improve the enforcement of social rights guaranteed by the Charter. In the first collective complaint lodged by the International Commission of Jurists against Portugal with regard to the special protection of children against physical and moral hazards (Article 7), the Committee found Portugal in violation of its obligations under the Charter.

91. What other standards, mechanisms and activities have been established by the Council of Europe?

The European Convention for the Prevention of Torture and Inhuman or Degrading Treatment or Punishment provides non-judicial preventative machinery to protect people deprived of their liberty. This is based on systematic monitoring and investigative visiting by independent experts of the Committee for the Prevention of Torture (CPT) (see Question 29). The Committee then makes recommendations (and may ultimately make a public statement) and reports annually to the Committee of Ministers.

The Council of Europe also places great importance on the issue of equality between women and men and combating racism and intolerance. The Steering Committee for Equality between Women and Men has taken action on issues such as violence against women and prostitution, and has also formulated concrete proposals following detailed analyses and conferences. In 1994, the concept of 'parity democracy' was launched, with the aim that women and men share in the decision-making process on an equal fifty-fifty basis. The European Commission against Racism and Intolerance (ECRI), which was set up in 1994, aims to assess the efficiency of national and international measures in combating racism and intolerance. ECRI looks at failures of implementation and, through a country-by-country approach, collects and circulates 'good examples' and works with national and local NGOs in awareness-raising sessions.

The Council of Europe is also involved in the field of the media. The aim is to strengthen and enhance freedom of expression and information and the right to seek, receive and impart information.

In the 1990s, the Council of Europe adopted two instruments in the field of protecting the rights of minorities: the European Charter on Regional and Minority Languages (1992) and the Framework Convention for the Protection of National Minorities (1995) (see Question 49). The Advisory Committee, established by the Framework Convention for the Protection of National Minorities, monitors the implementation of the Convention by the States Parties and adopts country-specific opinions, which are

submitted to the Committee of Ministers. The Advisory Committee comprises 18 independent experts. It examines the State Reports and has also developed the practice of carrying out regular country visits.

In 2005, the Council of Europe adopted the Convention on Action against Trafficking in Human Beings, which entered into force on February 2008. The Convention provides for a monitoring mechanism which consists of two pillars: The Group of Experts on Action against Trafficking in Human Beings (GRETA), a technical body composed of independent experts, and the Committee of the Parties, a political body comprising the representatives of the Parties to the Convention. The Committee of the Parties elected the members for the first composition of GRETA at their first meeting held in Strasbourg on 5 and 8 December 2008.[108]

The European Commission for Democracy through Law, known as the Venice Commission, is the Council of Europe advisory body on constitutional matters. Since its establishment in 1990, the Venice Commission aims at upholding the principles of democracy, human rights and the rule of law. The Commission works in the following fields: providing legal advice to Member States, assisting in electoral legislation and observing elections, cooperating with constitutional courts and further improving the functioning of democratic institutions.

The Council of Europe Commissioner for Human Rights is an independent institution, established by the Committee of Ministers in 1999 and mandated to promote the awareness of and respect for human rights among the Council of Europe Member States. The Commissioner carries out country visits and issues reports on the human rights situation which are presented to the Committee of Ministers and the Parliamentary Assembly of the Organization. The Commissioner also issues thematic recommendations on various human rights issues and aims to promote awareness of human rights and the empowerment of the national human rights institutions in the Member States.

92. Are the promotion and protection of human rights included in the treaties of the European Union?

The European Union (EU) was established on 1 November 1993, following the entry into force of the Treaty on European Union (TEU, Treaty of Maastricht). The European Community (EC), previously called the European Economic Community (EEC), which was created by the Treaty of Rome in 1957, is, since the Treaty of Maastricht, the largest structure of the European Union. The European Union is considered as the roof of a three pillar construction, where the EC is the first pillar, the Common Foreign and Security Policy (CFSP) the second pillar and the Cooperation in Justice and Home Affairs the third pillar.

The Treaty establishing the European Community (TEC) made no explicit reference to human rights and fundamental freedoms. However, the policies adopted by the Community institutions and the Heads of Member States reflected the principles of liberty, democracy and respect for human rights and fundamental freedoms, which are common to all Member States. In particular, the Court of Justice of the European Union recognized that these principles are part of community law, thereby ensuring that human rights are fully taken into account in the administration of justice.

In 1987, human rights were introduced into the Treaties for the first time in the preamble to the Single European Act (SEA). The Treaty of Maastricht (adopted in 1992) incorporated these principles into provisions contained in the body of the Treaty. The Treaty considers as one of the objectives of the Common Foreign and Security Policy of the EU the development and consolidation of 'democracy and the rule of law, and respect for human rights and fundamental freedoms' (Article 11, TEU). At the same time a new title on development cooperation included a second direct reference to human rights and democratization by stating that policy in this field 'shall contribute to the general objective of developing and consolidating democracy and the rule of law and that of respecting human rights and fundamental freedoms' (Article 177, TEC).

The Treaty of Amsterdam, which came into force on 1 May 1999, reaffirms in its Article 6 that the EU 'is founded on the

principles of liberty, democracy, respect for human rights and fundamental freedoms and the rule of law, principles that are common to all Member States'. Article 49 of the Treaty emphasizes that respect for these principles is also required by countries who apply for EU membership. A mechanism to sanction serious and persistent breaches of human rights by EU Member States is provided for in Article 7 of the Treaty. This particular provision was reinforced by the Treaty of Nice in December 2000.

The Amsterdam Treaty also contains a general clause on combating discrimination, provisions on measures concerning asylum, refugees and immigration, and certain competences in the field of employment, working conditions and social protection.

On 1 March 2007, the European Union Agency for Fundamental Rights (FRA) came into being. Based in Vienna, this body of the EU has the purpose of providing the relevant EU institutions and authorities, as well as Member States, with assistance and expertise relating to human rights.

93. What are the main components of the EU's external human rights policy?

The main EU initiatives in the field of human rights, in relation to third countries, consist of actions by the EC (first pillar) on the one hand, and the Common Foreign and Security Policy (second pillar) on the other hand.

Since 1992, the EC (which now forms one of the main pillars of the EU) has included in its bilateral trade and cooperation agreements with third countries a so-called human rights clause, which stipulates that respect for human rights and democracy constitutes an 'essential element' of the agreement. In event of a breach, the agreement may be suspended. However, the emphasis lies on promoting dialogue and positive measures rather than punitive action. Examples of agreements incorporating this provision include the Euro-Mediterranean Association Agreements and the Cotonou Agreement (ex-Lomé Convention) signed with African, Caribbean and Pacific (ACP) States in June 2000.

Under the European Instrument for Democracy and Human Rights (EIDHR) (replacing the 'European Initiative for Democracy

and Human Rights' in 2006), funds are allocated to support actions in the areas of human rights, democratization and conflict prevention. The budget for 2007-2013 is EUR 1.104 million, to be managed by the Commission assisted by a human rights and democracy committee.[109] The EIDHR is specifically aimed at NGOs, in recognition of their important contribution to the promotion of human rights and democracy. It is complementary to other EC external assistance programmes carried out with governments (Phare, Thacis, etc.) since it can be implemented with various partners, particularly NGOs and international organizations, without the host government's consent.

Common strategies, common positions and joint actions are the main legal instruments of the EU's Common Foreign and Security Policy. A significant number of them are focused on human rights and democratization or contain substantial human rights elements. Since 2003, the European Union has developed the practice of deploying missions under the European Security and Defence Policy (ESDP). These missions, which are located in various parts of the world and aim to promote global security, are guided by the 'Council Document on Mainstreaming Human Rights across CFSP and other EU policies' adopted on 13 November 2006.[110] Currently, human rights offices or experts are sent along with the missions in order to assure the promotion of the EU human rights agenda.

The EU's Annual report on Human Rights serves as a basis for making the EU's human rights policy more effective and consistent and gives an overview of all the human rights-related common strategies, common positions and joint actions. Furthermore, the EU adopted the Guidelines on Human Rights Dialogues in December 2001, which pledge the EU to raise the issues of human rights, democracy and the rule of law in all meetings with third countries and set out conditions for the conduct of specific human rights dialogues. Since then, the Council of the EU has issued a series of human rights guidelines which serve as a framework for the protection and promotion of human rights in third countries. In 2008, the Council issued guidelines on: violence against women and girls and combating all forms of discrimination against them; on the death penalty; on torture and on human rights defenders.

In addition, démarches to the authorities of third countries, often carried out in a confidential manner, are used to convey

concerns relating to human rights. The EU can also make public declarations, calling upon a government or other parties to respect human rights, or welcoming positive developments.

94. What is the purpose of the Charter of Fundamental Rights of the European Union?

Pursuant to the call by the European Councils of the Heads of State and Government in Cologne and Tampere in June and October 1999, a Charter of Fundamental Rights of the European Union was drafted and solemnly proclaimed at the European Council in Nice in December 2000. The Charter is intended to guide the action of the EU institutions in the field of human rights, to make these rights more visible and to promote citizens' awareness of their rights. The scope of the Charter is defined in Article 51(1). It is 'addressed to the institutions and bodies of the Union, with due regard to the principle of subsidiarity and to the Member States only when they are implementing Union law.' The Charter does not bind the Member States in areas of their national competence.

The Charter is, to a large extent, modelled on the provisions of the European Convention on Human Rights and contains seven chapters. Chapter I (Dignity) includes rights concerning the life and integrity of persons, such as the prohibition of torture. Chapter II (Freedoms) contains the right to respect for private life, the right to freedom of expression, religion and association, and the right to education, property and asylum. Chapter III (Equality) includes provisions on non-discrimination, cultural diversity, equality between men and women and the rights of children, older people and disabled persons. Chapter IV (Solidarity) contains the right to information and various labour rights, as well as provisions on health care and environmental protection. Chapter V (Citizen's Rights) includes voting and administrative rights and Chapter VI (Justice) includes the right to a fair trial and an effective legal redress. Finally, Chapter VII contains General Provisions concerning the status and scope of the Charter.

The status of the Charter is, at the present time, that of a Declaration. This means that, formally, it has no legally binding force. In 2008, the treaty of Lisbon amendments were not ratified.

Hence by May 2009, it had not yet entered into force. Nevertheless, since its proclamation, it has had an important influence on the judgements of the European Court of Justice, as well as on policies of the EU institutions.

95. What human rights instruments were adopted by the Organization of African Unity and subsequently by the African Union?

The Assembly of the Heads of State and Government of the Organization of African Unity (OAU) adopted the African Charter on Human and Peoples' Rights on 26 June 1981. It came into force in October 1986. As of 31 May 2009, it had been ratified by all fifty-three Member States of the African Union. Other human rights instruments adopted by the OAU are the Convention Governing the Specific Aspects of Refugee Problems in Africa, adopted in 1969 and in force since 1974, and the African Charter on the Rights and Welfare of the Child, adopted in 1990 and in force since 1999. In July 2003, the African Union adopted a Protocol on the Rights of Women in Africa. The Protocol is a significant step in the efforts to promote respect for the rights of women. It calls for, *inter alia*, the elimination of all forms of violence against women in Africa and the promotion of equality between women and men. At a meeting of Heads of fifty-three African States on 11 July 2000 the Constitutive Act of the African Union was agreed upon. It replaced the Organization of African Unity by the African Union and entered into force in July 2002.[111]

In 2007, the African Charter on Democracy, Elections and Governance was adopted by the African Union, in an effort to promote the principle of democracy throughout the continent. As of 31 May 2009, the Charter has not yet taken effect.[112] Another important instrument is the African Youth Charter, which was adopted in 2006 but as at 31 May 2009 had not yet entered into force. The Charter creates a legally binding framework for governments to develop supportive policies and programmes for young people.[113]

96. What rights are protected by the African Charter on Human and Peoples' Rights?

The Charter, inspired by the United Nations Charter and the Universal Declaration of Human Rights, has several elements that distinguish it from other international and regional human rights instruments. Uniquely, the Charter covers economic, social and cultural rights as well as civil and political rights, thus emphasizing that all human rights are indivisible and interdependent. Moreover, the Charter also promotes 'peoples' rights', in other words, the collective rights of people as a group. Linked with the principle of peoples' rights is the belief that human beings can only realize their full potential as members of communities. As such, human beings not only have rights but also responsibilities to communities, for example, duties towards the family, society, the State and the international community. The Charter charges States with the duty to ensure the exercise of the right to development.

97. What mechanisms have been established to implement the African Charter?

An African Commission on Human and Peoples' Rights was established in 1987, under the Charter, to promote human and peoples' rights and ensure their protection in Africa. This Commission, which is based in Banjul, the Gambia, has eleven members, selected on the basis of personal integrity and competence, who serve in their personal capacities and not as government representatives. The Commission has a number of functions, including the protection of the rights laid down in the Charter, and the promotion of discussion and development of those rights.

The African Commission examines periodic reports from States Parties on their compliance with the provisions of the Charter and establishes dialogue with State representatives, aimed at encouraging States to implement their human rights obligations.

Visits are undertaken by individual Commissioners to States Parties for purposes of promoting human rights. The Commission also issues interpretative statements on specific provisions of the Charter aimed at 'solving legal problems relating to human and

peoples' rights and fundamental freedoms upon which African Governments may base their legislation'. Statements have been issued on subjects such as the right to a fair trial and respect for humanitarian law. The two annual sessions of the Commission are held, not only at headquarters, but in other African countries, so that the work of the Commission may become widely known.

The Commission has appointed Special Rapporteurs on Extra-judicial Executions, Conditions of Prisons and Detention Centres, the Rights of Women, Freedom of Expression, Human Rights Defenders and Refugees and Displaced Persons. It has also created Working Groups on the following subjects: Indigenous Populations, Economic, Social and Cultural Rights, the Death Penalty, the Robben Island Guidelines and on Specific Issues. It has sent missions of investigation or monitor to States Parties where the human rights situation is of serious concern.

The 1998 Protocol to establish an African Court on Human and Peoples' Rights entered into force in 2004. In January 2006, the Executive Council of the African Union elected the first eleven Judges of the Court. Individuals and NGOs with observer status before the Commission can bring cases before the Court on violations of the rights enshrined in the Charter and on violations of human rights instruments ratified by the State in question. In 2008, by a new Protocol on the Statute of the African Court of Justice and Human Rights, the African Court on Human and Peoples' Rights is to be merged with the African Court of Justice. As at 31 May 2009 the new Protocol had not yet entered into force.[114]

98. Can States and/or individuals submit complaints to the African Commission on Human Rights?

The Charter is unique in that all States Parties must automatically accept the competence of the Commission to receive complaints of alleged violations of the rights under the Charter. Such complaints may be filed by States Parties as well as by individuals and non-governmental organizations, provided that the alleged violator has ratified the Charter. The entire procedure is confidential, but a summary of cases that have been considered is published in the

Commission's Annual Report.[115] The Commission prepares a report on its facts, findings and recommendations, which is sent to the State concerned and to the Assembly of the Heads of State and Government of the African Union. The latter may decide to make the findings public.[116]

This procedure also provides for provisional measures (urgent appeals) to be addressed to a State, which aim at preventing irreparable damage being caused to victim(s) of alleged violations of the Charter, pending the consideration of the complaint by the Commission.

99. What human rights instruments have been established by the Organization of American States (OAS)?

The OAS[117], created in 1948, is the oldest regional organization in the world and is comprised of thirty-five Member States, specifically, all the independent States in the Western hemisphere, from Canada to Chile. In 1948, the American Declaration of the Rights and Duties of Man was adopted. Although not legally binding as a Declaration, comparable to the Universal Declaration of Human Rights, most of the provisions in the American Declaration have become binding as international customary law. Although the OAS Charter and the American Declaration had already foreseen the establishment of an Inter-American Commission on Human Rights, it was not established until 1959 'to promote respect for and defence of human rights'. At first, the Commission was not permitted to consider individual complaints. In 1965, however, the mandate of the Commission was expanded to include individual complaints.

In 1969, the American Convention on Human Rights was adopted. It entered into force in July 1978.[118] The American Convention defined two organs for its supervision: the existing Inter-American Commission on Human Rights and the Inter-American Court on Human Rights. As the Inter-American Commission was established by the OAS Charter, the Commission may consider complaints concerning non-States Parties to the Convention regarding alleged violations of the rights set out in the American Declaration.

Two additional Protocols to the American Convention on Human Rights have also been adopted, one in the area of economic, social and cultural rights, known as the 'Protocol of San Salvador' and the second on the abolition of the death penalty, which entered into force respectively on 16 November 1999 and 28 August 1991. Other human rights treaties adopted by the OAS Member States include the Inter-American Convention to Prevent and Punish Torture, which entered into force on 28 February 1987; the Inter-American Convention on Forced Disappearance of Persons, which entered into force on 28 March 1996; the Inter-American Convention on the Elimination of All Forms of Discrimination against Persons with Disabilities, which entered into force on 14 September 2001; and the Inter-American Convention on the Prevention, Punishment and Eradication of Violence against Women, known as the 'Convention of Belem do Para', after the Brazilian city where it was adopted on 9 June 1994. These last two treaties were the first two international human rights treaties to deal with these issues.

100. What is the mandate of the Inter-American Commission on Human Rights?

The Commission, established by the Charter of the OAS, comprises seven members and is located at the headquarters of the OAS in Washington, D.C. It has two main functions: 1) to examine and decide upon petitions alleging violations of human rights by Member States, which are parties to the American Convention on Human Rights, and pursuant to the American Declaration on the Rights and Duties of Man, by Member States that are not parties to the American Convention and 2) to carry out on-site visits to Member States when it considers it advisable to do so and to prepare reports on those visits.

Due to the political changes in the region, the nature of the cases presented to the Commission tends to focus more on the inadequacies of the systems of the Member States rather than the pattern of gross and systematic violations that dominated in the past. Questions of due process and access to courts, freedom of expression, and the failure to investigate, try and punish, dominate the

current agenda. Consequently, in order to deal with issues that the Commission designates as being worthy of special attention, it created a number of Rapporteurs, in particular, a full-time Rapporteur on Freedom of Expression. In addition, members of the Commission serve as Rapporteurs for other important issues, such as the rights of women, children, indigenous people, migrant workers, internally displaced persons and prisoners. The Rapporteurs attend conferences, carry out on-site visits and present reports to the plenary on their topic of interest. A Unit for Human Rights Defenders has been created at the headquarters of the Commission. In 2007, the following Rapporteurs were operative: on rights of Indigenous Peoples, rights of Women, rights of Children, rights of Persons Deprived of Liberty in the Americas, rights of Afro-Descendents and against Racial Discrimination and rights of Migrant Workers and their Families. If a State does not comply with its decision, the Commission refers the case to the Inter-American Court on Human Rights, unless the majority of the Commission votes against this. In that case, the Commission represents the plaintiffs. By repeatedly presenting reports on the human rights violations committed primarily by non-democratic governments to the political organs of the OAS, the Commission played a crucial role in the resulting condemnation of these practices by the Member States. In 2007, the Commission received 1456 complaints on violations of the rights enshrined in the Convention and sent 11 applications to the Court.

101. What is the role of the Inter-American Court on Human Rights?

The Inter-American Court on Human Rights, which consists of seven members, was created as a result of the entry into force of the American Convention, and has its seat in San José, Costa Rica. As of 31 May 2009, there were twenty-four States Parties to the Convention and twenty-one of those States had also recognized the compulsory jurisdiction of the Court.[119]

In recent years the Commission and Court have created important jurisprudence as regards the incompatibility of 'amnesty' laws with a State's obligations under the Convention. These amnesty laws were adopted in many countries in the Americas to

block prosecution of members of the security forces or members of governments for human rights violations committed during military dictatorships. The counter-insurgency tactics of many security forces during the 1970s and 1980s resulted in the disappearance, torture and arbitrary detention of thousands of people. The courts in Argentina, for example, have cited the jurisprudence of the inter-American system in repealing their own amnesty laws.

In addition, the Commission and Court have issued important decisions as regards the right of indigenous groups in Nicaragua to collectively own property; the right to life of 'street children' in Guatemala; the right of civilians not to be tried by military courts in Peru; and the right of suspected terrorists to trials that afford them all the guarantees of due process. The Court has also established the right to reparations for victims of human rights violations, which includes not only monetary compensation for material and moral damages and costs and expenses, but also the right to have the State investigate, judge and punish those responsible for the violations of their rights.

102. How does the Organization for Security and Co-operation in Europe (OSCE) contribute to the promotion and protection of human rights?

The Organization for Security and Co-operation in Europe (OSCE) began its activities in the 1970s, under the name of the Conference on Security and Cooperation in Europe (CSCE), as a multilateral forum for dialogue and negotiation between East and West. It was renamed in 1995. In the Helsinki Final Act, signed in 1975, the Participating States[120] agreed on basic principles for behaviour among the States and of governments towards their citizens. The States also agreed to further development of the CSCE process in three main areas: questions relating to security in Europe; cooperation in the fields of economics, science and technology, and the environment; and cooperation in humanitarian and other fields. At successive follow-up meetings, participating States have made commitments to standards and norms on human rights and fundamental freedoms, ranging from the treatment of minorities

to prevention of torture, gender issues, protection of freedom of expression and abolition of the death penalty. Currently, human rights issues are being promoted and addressed by the OSCE Human Dimension of Security, as a part of the Organization's comprehensive concept of security.

Moreover, in the Final Document of the 1991 Moscow Conference on the Human Dimension of the OSCE, it was stated that commitments undertaken under the human dimension of the OSCE are matters of direct and legitimate concern of all Participating States and do not belong exclusively to the internal affairs of the State concerned. This commitment has been reiterated in subsequent undertakings.

Decisions within the OSCE are made on the basis of consensus (with a notable exception in the case of a clear and gross violation of OSCE commitments relating to human rights and fundamental freedoms, e.g. the suspension of Yugoslavia from the CSCE in 1992). All participating States have an equal status and decisions are politically binding. The annual Ministerial Council Meetings and the Permanent Council of the Organization have made decisions on human rights issues, including combating trafficking in human beings, empowering the rule of law in the OSCE area, promoting Roma and Sinti rights and fighting against discrimination. The Annual Human Dimension Meetings have consistently addressed human rights issues.

The OSCE provides active support where needed for the promotion of democracy, the rule of law and respect for human rights throughout the OSCE area. It has extensive activities in all phases of conflict, and other field activities within its area.

103. What human rights activities have been undertaken by the Organization for Security and Co-operation in Europe (OSCE)?

The High Commissioner for National Minorities, established by the OSCE, responds, at the earliest possible stage, to ethnic tensions that have the potential to develop into a conflict within the OSCE region. The mission of the High Commissioner is to try to contain and de-escalate such tension and to alert the OSCE. The High

Commissioner operates independently, preserving impartiality and confidentiality at all times. This work constitutes an essential contribution to the OSCE's preventive diplomacy for ensuring peace and stability in Europe.

The Office of Democratic Institutions and Human Rights (ODIHR) furthers human rights, democracy and the rule of law by providing a forum for addressing the States' implementation of their Human Dimension commitments. The ODIHR offers a framework for exchanging information on building democratic institutions and co-ordinates the monitoring of elections and the provision of advice and assistance in this regard. The Chairman-in-Office, being responsible for executive action in the OSCE, may also direct personal representatives to investigate specific human rights situations.

A Representative on Freedom of Media was appointed in 1998 with the objective of assisting participating States in further-ing free, independent and pluralistic media.

A significant aspect of the work of the OSCE in attempting to resolve problems in situations of conflict, potential conflict and post-conflict rehabilitation is reflected in its field operations. The mandates, composition, size and operations of long-term missions and other field activities vary. The central task, however, for all missions are Human Dimension issues, democracy and building the rule of law. At present the major missions are in Kosovo, Bosnia and Herzegovina, Croatia and Albania. OSCE missions and other field activities in various capacities are located in a number of other areas, such as Eastern Europe, Central Asia and the Caucasus.

104. Are there any initiatives being taken to establish other regional human rights systems?

Since 1993 the issue of appropriate regional machinery on human rights has been on the agenda of the Ministerial Meeting of the Association of South East Asian Nations (ASEAN). Parallel to this a Working Group for an ASEAN Human Rights Mechanism, formed by representatives of civil society, has been working towards the promotion of such a mechanism and submitted a draft Agreement

as a working document to the ASEAN Foreign Ministries in 2000. Article 14 of the ASEAN Charter, which was adopted in November 2007, calls for the creation of an ASEAN human rights body (AHRB) to protect and promote human rights. The High Level Panel (HLP) on the establishment of this body held its first meeting during the 41st ASEAN Ministerial Meeting in Singapore in July 2008. On 11 September 2008, the Working Group submitted its recommendations for the mandate and powers of the AHRB to the High Level Panel. The ASEAN Charter came into force in December 2008.

The Arab Charter on Human Rights was adopted by the Council of the League of Arab States on 15 September 1994.[121] The text has not been ratified, and hence is not operative. On 22 May 2004, a revised Arab Charter on Human Rights was adopted by the League of Arab States. The Charter entered into force on 15 March 2008.

The Organization of the Islamic Conference adopted the Cairo Declaration on Human Rights in Islam on 5 August 1990.

The role of civil society and the private sector in the field of human rights

105. What role do non-governmental organizations (NGOs) play in the promotion of human rights?

The role of NGOs in the promotion of human rights at international, regional and national levels is widely recognized and endorsed by the international community. NGOs contribute significantly to the United Nations human rights programme and have actively participated in major conferences in the field of human rights. They serve as a unique source of information; assist in the identification and drafting of new international standards; seek to obtain redress for victims of human rights abuses; and

play an important role in promoting human rights education, particularly at the non-formal level.

There are numerous NGOs, international and national, which are very active in the field of human rights. ECOSOC is authorized to consult with NGOs that deal with its areas of competence and, as of 31 May 2009, 3172 NGOs had been granted consultative status with ECOSOC.[122] As at 31 May 2009, 310 international NGOs and 19 foundations had official relations with UNESCO, while about 200 NGOs had consultative status with ILO.

The World Conference on Human Rights (1993) recognized the important role of non-governmental organizations in the promotion of all human rights and in humanitarian activities at national, regional and international levels. The Conference, in particular, expressed appreciation of their contribution to increasing public awareness of human rights issues, to education, training and research in this field, and to the process of standard setting. It furthermore pointed out that activities of NGOs should not be contrary to the purposes of the United Nations. NGOs should be free to carry out their human rights activities without interference, provided that they do so within the framework of national law and the Universal Declaration of Human Rights.[123] The 2005 World Summit under-

lined the importance of the contribution of NGOs in the promotion and implementation of development and human rights programmes (Outcome Document of the 2005 World Summit, General Assembly Resolution 60/1 of 24 October 2005).

The Office of the High Commissioner for Human Rights recognized the critical contributions made to the promotion and protection of human rights by NGOs and has emphasized that human rights defenders are 'crucial partners in the implementation of the universal human rights agenda'. The OHCHR established a post of NGO Liaison Officer in order to facilitate the interaction of NGOs with OHCHR (2004). The OHCHR published a handbook for civil society actors in order to promote cooperation of the UN with NGOs and civil society (2008).

106. What role do national human rights institutions play in the promotion of human rights?

The creation of national human rights institutions has been accorded increasing priority in light of their significant contribution to the effective implementation of international human rights standards. Their important and constructive role in the promotion and protection of human rights was reaffirmed in the Vienna Declaration and Programme of Action adopted by the World Conference on Human Rights in 1993.

An international workshop held in Paris in October 1991 put forward a set of recommendations on the role, composition, status and functions of national institutions, commonly known as the Paris Principles. The Paris Principles, subsequently endorsed by the UN General Assembly (annex to resolution 48/134 of 20 December 1993) have become the reference point for the establishment and operation of national human rights institutions.

According to these Principles, the mandate of a national institution, whether emanating from the constitution or a legislative text, shall be as broad as possible and shall extend, *inter alia*, to the following responsibilities: to submit to governments, parliaments, and any other competent authority, on an advisory basis, opinions, recommendations, proposals and reports; to promote and ensure the

harmonization of national legislation, regulations and practices with international human rights law; to contribute to the State reports to United Nations bodies; to disseminate information on human rights; and to contribute to human rights education. Such an institution may also be authorized to hear and consider complaints and petitions concerning individual situations. Particular attention is attached to the pluralism and independence of national institutions, which are inextricably linked to the selection of its members, the stability of its mandate, and the methods of operation, including adequate investigative powers, as well as to the infrastructure and resources available to it.

The majority of existing national institutions can be grouped together in two broad categories: 'human rights commissions' and 'ombudsmen'. Another less common, but no less important, variety are the 'specialized' national institutions which function to protect the rights of a particular vulnerable group, such as ethnic and linguistic minorities, indigenous populations, children, refugees and women.

The United Nations and in particular the Office of the United Nations High Commissioner for Human Rights are playing a catalytic role, assisting States in the establishment of national human rights institutions, and providing support to the work of these institutions.

In 1993, the International Coordinating Committee (ICC) of National Institutions for the Promotion and Protection of Human Rights was established with the purpose of supporting the creation and strengthening of national human rights institutions in conformity with the Paris Principles, and reinforcing coordination and cooperation among the national institutions, as well as with OHCHR and other United Nations bodies and agencies. In 1998, the ICC developed its rules of procedure and enlarged its membership to 16 members. The Sub-Committee on Accreditation to the ICC is responsible for the accreditation of the National Human Rights Institutions (NHRI) and for making recommendations on their compliance with the Paris Principles. As of December 2008, there were 64 NHRIs accredited with A status to the ICC.

The Ninth International Conference of the National Human Rights Institutions was held in Nairobi in October 2008, in which more than 120 representatives from NHRIs participated.

107. Do corporations have human rights obligations?

Traditionally, international human rights law has been concerned with the responsibility of States to protect and promote human rights. Globalization and the search for international competitive advantages have strengthened the role and power of some transnational corporations in comparison with States. The power of transnational corporations should, however, not be exercised without due consideration of human rights.

These concerns have been taken up in international forums. The Rio Declaration and the Copenhagen Declaration[124] have underscored the responsibilities of Transnational Corporations (TNC) with regard to development and the protection of the environment. It is increasingly recognized that TNCs have an important role to play in the promotion and protection of human rights. The 'Global Compact' initiative proposed by the Secretary-General of the United Nations in January 1999 is not a regulatory instrument or a code of conduct, but a value-based platform designed to promote good practices based on universal principles.

The Compact encompasses nine principles, drawn from international instruments including the Universal Declaration of Human Rights, the ILO's Fundamental Principles on Rights at Work and the Rio Principles on Environment and Development.[125] These principles encourage countries to support and respect the protection of international human rights within their sphere of influence; make sure their own corporations are not complicit in human rights abuses; permit freedom of association and the effective recognition of the right to collective bargaining; eliminate of all forms of forced and compulsory labour; secure the effective abolition of child labour; eliminate of discrimination in respect to employment and occupation; support a precautionary approach to environmental challenges; undertake initiatives to promote greater environmental responsibility; and encourage the development and diffusion of environmentally friendly technologies. It represents an important step towards voluntary cooperation between the private sector and the United Nations toward attaining responsible corporate impact on the enjoyment of human rights. In addition, companies and industry-specific associations of companies (such as

those in the apparel industry) are increasingly adopting voluntary codes of conduct or entering into partnerships with NGOs and other groups to develop codes of conduct and principles of monitoring, addressing human rights, labour rights and environmental concerns. Under the Global Compact a Governance Framework was established to promote the principles of the Compact, which was renewed in August 2005. Under the Framework there are the following entities: the Global Compact Leaders Summit; the Local Networks; the Annual Local Networks Forum; the Board; the Global Compact Office; the Inter-Agency Team; and the Donor Group.

In 2005, the High Commissioner for Human Rights presented to the Commission on Human Rights a report on the responsibilities of transnational corporations and related business enterprises with regard to human rights (E/CN.4/2005/91, 15 February 2005). On 15 February 2005 the Commission (replaced by the Human Rights Council in 2006), asked the Secretary-General to appoint a Special Representative on Human Rights and Transnational Corporations and Other Business Enterprises for an initial period of two years. The Special Representative's main responsibilities were: to identify and clarify standards of corporate responsibility and accountability for transnational corporations and other business enterprises with regard to human rights; to elaborate on the role of States in effectively regulating and adjudicating the role of transnational corporations and other business enterprises with regard to human rights; to research and clarify the implications for transnational corporations and other business enterprises of concepts such as 'complicity' and 'sphere of influence'; to develop materials and methodologies for undertaking human rights impact assessments of the activities of transnational corporations and other business enterprises. The Special Representative's mandate was renewed by the Human Rights Council in 2008 for three years.

Human rights education

108. What role does human rights education play in the promotion and protection of human rights?

The awareness of a person's own rights and of the rights of others is an indispensable precondition for the effective implementation of human rights. Knowledge of human rights standards and mechanisms for their protection empowers people so as to be able to claim and assert their own rights, as well as the rights of others.

The importance of education for the promotion of respect for human rights and the consolidation of peace was affirmed in the Universal Declaration of Human Rights, which stated that education shall 'be directed to the full development of the human personality and to the strengthening of respect for human rights and fundamental freedoms' (Article 26). Based on this provision, as well as on the provisions of other international human rights instruments addressing human rights education, the Plan of Action of the UN Decade for Human Rights Education (1995–2004) defined human rights education as 'training, dissemination and information efforts aimed at the building of a universal culture of human rights through the imparting of knowledge and skills and the moulding of attitudes.'[126] Furthermore, human rights education should be in conformity with the principle of indivisibility, interdependence, interrelation and equal importance of all human rights – civil, cultural, economic, political and social.

The World Programme on Human Rights Education (2005- ongoing) and the International Year of Human Rights Learning (2009) further underline the importance of human rights education for the promotion and protection of human rights (see Question 109).

109. What measures have been taken by the United Nations system to promote human rights education?

The United Nations General Assembly, recognizing the importance of improving public knowledge in the field of human rights, launched, on 10 December 1988, a World Public Information Campaign for Human Rights (Resolution 43/128). The aim of this campaign was to develop programmes of teaching, education and information in the field of human rights in a global and practically oriented manner. Features in the campaign included the production and dissemination of printed material on human rights, tailored both to regional and national requirements; the organization of workshops and seminars; the granting of fellowships; and the creation of national human rights institutions. Special attention was also paid to the media in order to increase public awareness of human rights.

The Vienna Declaration and Programme of Action (1993), taking account of the World Plan of Action on Education for Human Rights and Democracy,[127] encourages States to strive to eradicate illiteracy, to include human rights, humanitarian law, democracy and the rule of law in all formal and non-formal educational curricula, and to develop programmes for ensuring the wide dissemination of public information. They are expected to take particular account of the human rights needs of women and children, as well as of persons belonging to minorities, indigenous peoples, migrants and elderly people. Human rights education is an integral part of certain United Nations peace-building operations, e.g. in El Salvador and Cambodia.

December 1994, the General Assembly proclaimed the ten-year period beginning on 1 January 1995 the United Nations Decade for Human Rights Education (1995–2004). The objectives of the Decade have been spelled out in the Plan of Action adopted by the General Assembly (para. 10). They include:

(a)   The assessment of needs and the formulation of effective strategies for the furtherance of human rights education at all school levels, in vocational training and formal, as well as non-formal, learning.

(b)   The building and strengthening of programmes and capacities for human rights education at the international, regional, national and local levels.

(c)   The coordinated development of human rights education materials.

(d)   The strengthening of the role and capacity of the mass media in the furtherance of human rights education.

(e)   The global dissemination of the Universal Declaration of Human Rights in the maximum possible number of languages and in other forms appropriate for various levels of literacy and for the disabled.

The General Assembly appealed to all governments 'to contribute to the implementation of the Plan of Action and to step up their efforts to eradicate illiteracy and to direct education towards the full development of the human personality and to the strengthening of respect for human rights and fundamental freedoms'. It urged governmental and non-governmental educational agencies to intensify their efforts to establish and implement programmes of human rights education, in particular by preparing and implementing national plans in this field.

United Nations specialized agencies and programmes, in particular UNESCO, were invited to collaborate closely among themselves and with OHCHR and to contribute, within their respective spheres of competence, to the implementation of the Plan of Action.

The General Assembly called upon international, regional and national non-governmental organizations, in particular those concerned with women, labour, development and the environment, as well as all other social justice groups, human rights advocates, educators, religious organizations and the media, to increase their involvement in formal and non-formal education in human rights.

An important momentum of the Decade was the celebration of the 50th anniversary of the Universal Declaration of Human Rights (10 December 1998). In 2000, the Office of the High Commissioner for Human Rights conducted jointly with UNESCO the Mid-Term Global Evaluation of the Decade. This study provided an overview of the progress made so far and helped

identify obstacles and challenges to the implementation of the Plan of Action of the Decade. The High Commissioner for Human Rights underlined, in her report on the mid-term evaluation of the Decade, the importance of the Decade as the sole mechanism for global mobilization of strategies for human rights education and advocated for the need for sustainability beyond the Decade.[128]

On 10 December 2004, the General Assembly proclaimed the World Programme for Human Rights Education with the aim of advancing the implementation of human rights education programmes in all sectors. The Programme started in 2005 and as of 31 May 2009 it was still ongoing. Based on the achievements of the Decade (1995-2004), the World Programme aims at promoting a common understanding of the basic principles and methodologies of human rights education. The Programme is structured in phases. The first phase of the Programme covers the period 2005-2009 and focuses on the primary and secondary school systems. The *Plan of Action* for the first phase proposes a concrete strategy and practical ideas for implementing human rights education at the national level.

In the World Summit of 2005 the Member States of the United Nations expressed their support for the promotion of human rights education and learning at all levels, including through the World Programme. They also encouraged all States to develop initiatives in the field of human rights education (2005 World Summit Outcome Document, Resolution 60/1, para. 131, 24 October 2005).

In December 2007, the General Assembly proclaimed the International Year of Human Rights Learning (Resolution 62/171 of 18 December 2007) which started on 10 December 2008. The Year aims to enhance the knowledge of all human rights, including the right to development. The Human Rights Council and the High Commissioner for Human Rights are requested, in cooperation with the Member States, civil society and all UN agencies, funds and programmes, to promote human rights learning 'at all levels of society'.

110. What initiatives have been taken by UNESCO in the area of human rights education (HRE)?

UNESCO has long-standing experience in the field of human rights education, a domain in which it has been active since its inception in 1945. HRE was addressed in the 1960 Convention against Discrimination in Education (Article 5) and was the subject of the Recommendation concerning Education for International Understanding, Cooperation and Peace and Education relating to Human Rights and Fundamental Freedoms (1978). The Recommendation establishes guiding principles for national education policies, discusses ethical, civic, cultural and other aspects of learning and training, and makes concrete proposals for action to promote HRE.

Other important instruments complementing the normative framework on HRE were the World Plan of Action on Education for Human Rights and Democracy, adopted by the International Congress on Education for Human Rights, and the Declaration (1994) and Integrated Framework of Action on Education for Peace, Human Rights and Democracy (1995).[129] Member States submit to UNESCO periodic reports on the implementation of these instruments.

From 1995 to 2004, UNESCO's activities in the area of human rights education took place within the framework of the United Nations Decade for Human Rights Education (1995–2004) and the relevant Plan of Action. The organization was acknowledged as a central actor in this respect and, working closely with OHCHR, was entrusted with the coordination of the activities of the Decade, for the attainment of the aims spelled out in the Plan of Action (see Question 109). UNESCO convened, in cooperation with OHCHR, five regional conferences on human rights education.[130] Their objective was to give an impetus to human rights education activities in each region through the promotion of regional ownership of HRE strategies.

The UNESCO Strategy on Human Rights, adopted in 2003, underlined human rights education as a priority area in UNESCO's action in the field of human rights (UNESCO Strategy on Human Rights, October 2003, Section II, para 24-29).[131]

Following the conclusion of the UN Decade on Human Rights Education, UNESCO has framed its Strategy on HRE under the UN World Programme on Human Rights Education and is playing a very active role in terms of international coordination of efforts (along with UNICEF, UNDP and OHCHR which is in charge of the overall Programme).

UNESCO promotes a holistic approach to human rights education. According to UNESCO, human rights education is an integral part of the right to education and 'is increasingly gaining

recognition as a human right itself'.[132] In this context, human rights are implemented at all levels of the educational system, and are taught through both content transmission and experiences. This approach involves not only the content of the curriculum but also the educational processes, the pedagogical methods and the environment within which education takes place, including school management. Thus, within this holistic approach, human rights education should constitute the basis for the democratization of educational systems in the context of national education reforms with a view to integrating the learning and practice of human rights.

UNESCO implements national and subregional pilot projects in a number of regions with a view to mainstreaming human rights education within the educational systems. These projects primarily focus on the revision of curricula and textbooks; the training of trainers, educators and administrative personnel in the educational system; and the production of educational materials for the training of both students and teachers. In the area of non-formal education, innovative methodologies of human rights education were tested through a series of social mobilization projects, integrating human rights with local development. UNESCO has also produced several documents, manuals and publications relating to human rights, as well as on human rights education.

In addition, UNESCO advocates human rights education through international and regional conferences and through the organization of national forums and workshops. UNESCO also maintains several networks in the area of human rights education, such as the Associated Schools Project Network, the network of UNESCO Chairs, the Network of Research and Training Institutions, an Electronic network on human rights education in Latin America and the UNESCO Education Server Programme for Civic and Human Rights Education in South East Europe. The International Centre for the Advancement of Human Rights was established in Buenos Aires, in February 2009, under the auspices of UNESCO. Promotion of human rights education is a main activity of the Centre. The UNESCO/Bilbao Prize for the Promotion of a Culture of Human Rights aims to reward the efforts of institutions, organizations and individuals in this field. This Prize is a successor of the UNESCO Prize for Human Rights Education, established in 1978 and awarded 15 times.

Contemporary challenges

111. What are the challenges of globalization to the realization of human rights?

While globalization has created unprecedented wealth and well-being, it has been accompanied by increasing poverty, inequality and exclusion for many countries, groups and individuals alike. In the words of the former UN Secretary-General, Kofi Annan, '... the pursuit of development, the engagement with globalization, and the management of change must all yield to human rights imperatives rather than the reverse'.[133] Globalization has brought about an expansion of the traditional approach to human rights in a number of ways.

First, development and poverty are increasingly being viewed from an international human rights perspective. Therefore issues such as foreign aid and debt and the impact of the international economic order on domestic social policies are now being debated in human rights terms. Such a human rights approach implies obligations and accountability of donor States.

Second, the focus of human rights law is expanding from traditional notions of exclusive State responsibility to include the obligations and responsibilities of non-State actors (such as international financial institutions and corporations) in promoting and protecting human rights.

Consequently, a basic understanding of the role of the various international institutions involved is indispensable. The main three institutions that have to be considered in this regard are: the World Bank, an intergovernmental organization that is the world's largest source of development assistance; the International Monetary Fund (IMF), which exercises surveillance over the exchange rate policies of its members through an evaluation of each country's economic and financial policies and attaches specific policy requirements as conditions for a loan to a country; and the World Trade Organization (WTO), an international, intergovernmental organization dealing with the rules of trade between nations.

The recent financial and economic crises have affected the lives of people all over the world. These crises have led to the increase of poverty and a setback in the promotion of development, especially in the framework of the achievement of the Millennium Development Goals (see Question 113). The impact and severity of this global crisis on the enjoyment of human rights has been recognized by the Human Rights Council (see Question 112) and the UN system in general.

However, this challenging situation presents an opportunity for the international community to address the weaknesses of the current system and reconsider its structure and values. Human rights need to be protected and special consideration needs to be given to the enjoyment of economic, social and cultural rights in the most affected regions.

112. How are the issues of globalization, the global financial and economic crises and human rights being addressed within the United Nations system?

In recent years there have been increasingly urgent calls from the General Assembly, the Commission on Human Rights and the Sub-Commission on Human Rights to explore the human rights dimensions of globalization. In 1999, the Commission on Human Rights (replaced by the Human Rights Council in 2006) recognized that globalization is not only an economic process but that it also has social, political, environmental, cultural and legal dimensions that affect human rights and may differ from country to country. Pursuant to this, the Sub-Commission appointed two Special Rapporteurs to undertake a study on the issue of globalization and its impact on the full enjoyment of human rights. A preliminary report was submitted, which called for a critical reconceptualization of policies and instruments of international trade, investment and finance. In 2000 the Commission on Human Rights established the mandate of the Independent Expert on the Effects of Foreign Debt and other related International Financial Obligations of States on the Full Enjoyment of Human Rights, Particularly Economic, Social and

Cultural Rights. The Expert's mandate was renewed in 2008 by the Human Rights Council, for a period of three years.

The Sub-Commission on Human Rights held a pre-sessional forum on economic, social and cultural rights in July 2002 known as the 'Social Forum'. The aim of the Social Forum was to discuss the most important issues affecting development in today's world, in particular those relating to globalization and its impact on people, poverty, development, cooperation and the full enjoyment of individual rights. Since then, four more 'Social Forums' have taken place. The 2008 Social Forum, took place in September 2008 (Human Rights Council Resolution 6/13).

The Committee on Economic, Social and Cultural Rights discussed the impact of globalization on economic, social and cultural rights on 11 May 1998, at a Day of General Discussion entitled 'Globalisation and its Impact on the Enjoyment of Economic and Social Rights'. It concluded that globalization has produced fundamental changes within all societies and that, while it is not incompatible with economic, social and cultural rights, it must be complemented by human rights norms to ensure that the importance of human rights not be neglected.

On 17 December 1998, the General Assembly convened the Millennium Summit of the United Nations and requested the Secretary-General to submit a report on globalization and its impact on the full enjoyment of all rights.[134] This report submitted at the fifty-fifth session (August 2000) of the General Assembly, is a comprehensive study of the effect of globalization. The study concludes that while globalization provides potential for the promotion and protection of human rights through economic growth, increased wealth, greater interconnection between peoples and cultures, and new opportunities for development, its benefits are not being enjoyed evenly. Further it notes that, while the goals and programmes are already formulated to deal properly with the problem, the strategy to achieve them lies in acknowledging that the principles and standards of human rights should be adopted as an indispensable framework for globalization.

The Human Rights Council recognized the gravity of the global financial and economic crises and the possible dangers related to the enjoyment of human rights. On 20-23 February 2009, it held a special session on the subject and issued a resolu-

tion (S-10/1, on 23 February 2009) on the Impact of the Global Economic and Financial Crises on the Universal Realization and Effective Enjoyment of Human Rights.[135] In this resolution, the HRC expresses the deep concern of its Members that human rights and development initiatives are affected by the crisis and calls for the special procedures mandate holders to consider and report any impact of the crises on human rights, especially economic, social and cultural rights, according to their respective mandates. It also requests from the UN treaty bodies to consider the impact of the crises and present relevant recommendations. The UN General Assembly decided to hold a high level conference (June 2009), on the global financial and economic crises and their impact on development. Other UN bodies and agencies have also considered the issue and held relevant meetings, seminars and reports, such as the WHO Report of a High-Level Consultation on the Financial Crisis and Global Health.

113. What are the key objectives of the United Nations Millennium Declaration?

At the conclusion of the UN Millennium Summit held from 6 to 8 September 2000, the General Assembly[136] adopted the United Nations Millennium Declaration, endorsed by the largest-ever gathering of world leaders. The Declaration reaffirms the role of the United Nations in the promotion of peace and human rights and identifies the regulation of globalization as an integral part of that process. The Declaration states that the central challenge of today is to ensure that globalization becomes a positive force for all the world's people. To do this the Declaration sets out fundamental values essential for the new globalized world. These are freedom, equality, tolerance, solidarity, respect for nature and shared responsibility. The Declaration identifies and assigns significance to key objective areas where these fundamental values must be translated: peace and security; development and poverty eradication; protecting our common environment; human rights, democracy and good governance; protecting the vulnerable; meeting the special needs of Africa; and strengthening the United Nations. It resolves to integrate these issues into all aspects of the work of the

United Nations. Implementing these goals within a human rights framework will ensure that they affect the most vulnerable members of society. Moreover this will provide an important opportunity for meaningful mainstreaming of human rights.

The Heads of State and Government have furthermore pledged to meet the so-called Millennium Development Goals. These Goals reflect global targets for reducing poverty and improving the lives of people. They include targets for 2015, such as halving extreme poverty and hunger, achieving universal primary education and creating a global partnership for development, as well as targets for aid, trade and debt relief.

Some progress has been achieved, as reflected by the 2008 Millennium Development Goals Report, especially in the fields of primary school enrolment, the gender parity index in primary education, access to safe drinking water, fighting malaria, AIDS and tuberculosis.[137]

114. What is meant by 'the right to development'?

The right to development was first recognized by the Commission on Human Rights in 1977 and then given further definition in 1986, when the General Assembly adopted a 'Declaration on the Right to Development'.[138] The Declaration states that the right is an 'inalienable human right by virtue of which every human person and all peoples are entitled to participate in, contribute to and enjoy economic, social and cultural development, in which all human rights and fundamental freedoms can be fully realized'. The Right also includes full sovereignty over natural resources, self-determination, popular participation in development and equality of opportunity. The Declaration places the primary responsibility on the State but also articulates a collective responsibility of all States for the creation of favourable international conditions for the realization of the Right and for the promotion of a new international order, based on interdependence and mutual interest.

It has been suggested that the right to development requires the provision of aid to developing countries and the elimination of oppressive debt burdens, which hinder the implementation of

economic, social and cultural rights. This continues to be an issue of debate.

The World Conference on Human Rights, held in Vienna in 1993, reaffirmed the universal and inalienable nature of the right to development and recognized that democracy, development and respect for human rights and fundamental freedoms are interdependent and mutually reinforcing. The Rio Declaration on Environment and Development (1992) placed 'human beings at the centre of concerns for sustainable development' and linked environmental concerns with the development process. The World Summits for Social Development (Copenhagen, 1995; Johannesburg, 2002) have also supported and further strengthened these linkages (see Part II, Article 28).

115. What are the main activities of the UN system concerning the right to development and sustainable development?

In 1998, a dual mechanism was established by the Commission on Human Rights, mandated by Decision 269 of ECOSOC, to explore in greater depth ways of implementing the right to development. For this purpose an open-ended Working Group on the Right to Development was set up and a high-level task force on the implementation of the right to development was established in 2004. It also appointed an Independent Expert on the Right to Development, whose mandate expired in 2005. The Independent Expert on Human Rights and International Solidarity (appointed in 2005 and renewed by the Human Rights Council in 2008 for three years) is dealing, *inter alia*, with the question of development. The Office of the High Commissioner for Human Rights is also responsible for promoting the right to development and enhancing support from relevant bodies of the United Nations system for that purpose.

The Secretary-General, in his agenda for reform of the United Nations,[139] designated human rights as a cross-cutting issue, which should be integrated into all areas of United Nations activity, including development and humanitarian action. The Office of the High Commissioner for Human Rights under this agenda has

been charged with mainstreaming human rights in development programming and it has set up a number of initiatives towards this end.

Leaders have also set Millennium Development Goals. The International Conference on Financing for Development, held in Monterrey, Mexico in 2002, confronted the challenges of financing for development. The Heads of State agreed to mobilize financial resources and achieve national and international economic conditions needed to fulfil internationally agreed development goals, including those contained in the Millennium Declaration. They also agreed to strengthen the United Nations as the main organization for rebuilding the international financial system, working with the World Bank, the IMF and the WTO.

At the World Summit on Sustainable Development held in Johannesburg in 2002, governments agreed to reaffirm a wide range of concrete commitments and targets for action to achieve more effective implementation of sustainable development objectives. The views of representatives of civil society were given prominence at the Summit in recognition of the role of civil society in implementing the outcomes and promoting partnership initiatives.

The Johannesburg Declaration on Sustainable Development and Plan of Implementation was subsequently endorsed by the General Assembly (December 2002). Sustainable development was acknowledged as a key element of the overarching framework of United Nations activities; in particular those activities for achieving internationally agreed development goals, such as in the United Nations Millennium Declaration.

The Follow-Up International Conference on Financing for Development, held in Doha in November-December 2008, reviewed the implementation of the Monterrey consensus. It issued the Doha Declaration on Financing for Development (A/CONF.212/L.1/REV 1, 9 December 2008), which reaffirmed the consensus obtained in Monterrey on Financing for Development and application of a more people-oriented approach to development.

116. How does the OHCHR promote the right to development?

The OHCHR supports both rights-based development practice and efforts to study the right to development, as well as the means of implementing this right.

As part of mainstreaming human rights within the United Nations system, the Office works with the United Nations Development Programme (UNDP) in building human rights capacities in UNDP development work on the ground in many countries. It has pioneered the development of human rights guidelines for integration into poverty reduction strategies and it works to promote economic, social and cultural rights in the context of development.

The OHCHR supports the Human Rights Council Special Procedures mandate holders and provides secretarial support to

the annual, pre-sessional working group of the Council on the right to development. In addition, it has worked with the Food and Agriculture Organization (FAO) and developed human rights guidelines on HIV/AIDS in partnership with UNAIDS. In 2008, the OHCHR published a booklet on the rights-based approach to development under the title 'Claiming the Millennium Development Goals: A Human Rights Approach'.[140]

117. What response to terrorism does international human rights law require?

Long before the terrorist attacks on 11 September 2001, the need for international cooperation to combat terrorist practices was acknowledged. The UN General Assembly adopted the Convention on the Prevention and Punishment of Crimes against Internationally Protected Persons, including Diplomatic Agents (1973), the International Convention against the Taking of Hostages (1979), the International Convention for the Suppression of Terrorist Bombings (1997) and the International Convention for the Suppression of the Financing of Terrorism (1999).

Moreover, several instruments against terrorism have been elaborated at the regional level. The Convention to Prevent and Punish the Acts of Terrorism taking the Forms of Crimes against Persons and Related Extortion that are of International Significance and the Inter-American Convention Against Terrorism were adopted by the Organization of American States (OAS) in 1971 and in 2002, respectively, and the European Convention on the Suppression of Terrorism was adopted by the Council of Europe in 1977. The League of Arab States adopted the Arab Convention on the Suppression of Terrorism (1998), the Organization of the Islamic Conference adopted the Convention on Combating International Terrorism (1999) and the African Union (formerly the Organization of African Unity) adopted the Convention on the Prevention and Combating of Terrorism (1999). In 2005, the International Convention for the Suppression of Acts of Nuclear Terrorism was adopted by the United Nations.

The common feature of all the above instruments is the absence of a general and comprehensive definition of terrorism.

They are limited to outlawing certain criminal acts whose inclusion in the concept of terrorism raised no objection at the time of their adoption. The provisions of these instruments create obligations only for States Parties; therefore, non-State actors, including armed groups, are not bound by them. However, any State may bring to justice any individual, regardless of organizational affiliation, who is responsible for terrorist acts, inasmuch as the acts constitute war crimes and crimes against humanity, under the principle of universal jurisdiction.

The direct linkage between terrorism and violations of human rights was recognized by the World Conference on Human Rights (Vienna, 1993). The Vienna Declaration and its Programme of Action affirm that 'the acts, methods and practices of terrorism in all its forms and manifestations as well as linkage in some countries to drug trafficking are activities aimed at the destruction of human rights, fundamental freedoms and democracy, threatening territorial integrity, security of States and destabilizing legitimately constituted Governments'. It concluded that 'the international community should take the necessary steps to enhance cooperation to prevent and combat terrorism'.

The United Nations General Assembly has repeatedly expressed in a number of resolutions (48/122, 49/185, 50/186, 52/133, 54/164) its unequivocal condemnation of the acts of terrorism.

The terrorist attacks of 11 September 2001 put the question of the prevention and elimination of terrorism at the top of the agenda of the international community. The Security Council unanimously adopted Resolutions 1368 (2001) and 1373 (2001) condemning terrorism. The latter Resolution established a Counter-Terrorism Committee, composed of all members of the Security Council, to monitor the implementation of the provisions of this Resolution. The General Assembly convened a special session in 2001 and adopted, by consensus, Resolution 56/1. In all the resolutions adopted since then by the Security Council and the General Assembly it was underlined that a shared international commitment is needed to find an effective, sustainable and multilateral response to the problem of terrorism. Moreover, the General Assembly noted the growing consciousness within the international community of the negative effects of terrorism on the full enjoyment of human

rights and the establishment of the rule of law and democratic freedoms.

In October 2001, the United Nations Secretary-General established the Policy Working Group on the United Nations and Terrorism. It was mandated to identify the longer-term implications and broad policy dimensions of terrorism for the United Nations and to formulate recommendations on the steps to be taken by the United Nations system to address the issue. In its report presented to the General Assembly in 2002 (Document A/57/273-S/2002/875), the Working Group stressed that terrorism is undermining and threatening the core principles and purposes of the United Nations Charter. It also stressed the necessity of intensifying efforts to combat violations of human rights, since terrorists often exploit human rights violations to gain support for their actions. It underlined that terrorism is an assault on basic rights. The Working Group, however, also emphasized that the fight against terrorism should be respectful of international human rights obligations. In Resolution 57/219 the General Assembly, recalling the provisions of Article 4 of ICCPR, according to which certain rights are non-derogable in any circumstances, affirmed that States must ensure that any measure taken to combat terrorism complies with their obligations under international law, in particular international human rights, refugee and humanitarian law. As the Secretary-General of the United Nations stressed, there can be no trade-off between effective action against terrorism and protection of human rights. A number of international organizations have urged States to ensure that any measure that restricts human rights strike a fair balance between legitimate national security concerns and fundamental freedoms and remain fully consistent with their international law commitments.[141] The United Nations system, regional intergovernmental organizations and a great number of organizations and institutions working in the field of human rights are paying increased attention to the issues linked with the struggle against terrorism. The Commission on Human Rights, as well as the Sub-Commission on Prevention of Discrimination and Protection of Minorities, has adopted several resolutions on human rights and terrorism. A Special Rapporteur of the Sub-Commission conducted a thorough study on the question of terrorism and human rights on 7 June 1999 (E/CN.4/Sub.2/1999/27).

In April 2005, the Commission on Human Rights established (Resolution 2005/80) the mandate of the Special Rapporteur on the Promotion and Protection of Human Rights while Countering Terrorism. The Rapporteur's mandate was renewed for three years by the Human Rights Council in 2007.

The United Nation's Global Counter-Terrorism Strategy, adopted by the United Nations in 2006, is the current platform for coordination of UN efforts on this subject. The Strategy underlines the need to defend human rights and promote the rule of law while countering terrorism.

Part II

The Universal Declaration of Human Rights
What each Article means

The first twenty-one Articles of the Declaration correspond, for the most part, to what are called civil and political rights and concern the freedom and personal security of individuals.

Article 1.
All human beings are born free and equal in dignity and rights. They are endowed with reason and conscience and should act towards one another in a spirit of brotherhood.

Does this mean that all people are equal?

To be born 'free' means that all people have an equal right to freedom, but we know they are affected throughout life by economic and social as well as civil and political restrictions. Freedom is not and cannot be total nor can the freedom of one person be at the expense of the freedom of others. Freedom, therefore, should not be equated with anarchy.

'Equal' does not mean that individuals are identical or similar in terms of physical or mental capabilities, talents and respective characteristics. Indeed, each individual is different from any other individual and the differences between individuals within any social or cultural group may be greater than the differences

between individuals of different social and cultural groups. There is no justification whatsoever for classifying groups hierarchically on the basis of any intellectual capacities or genetic characteristics. Discrimination and denial on grounds of 'race' or anti-social beliefs of innate inequality between differing social or ethnic groups have absolutely no scientific foundation. Denying persons, on the basis of the groups to which they belong, the possibility of developing their full potential as individuals is a grave injustice and a negation of their right to equality and dignity.

This Article also recalls the duty of everyone to treat other people in a 'spirit of brotherhood', that is, as fellow human beings, equal in rights and dignity.

The practice of tolerance is the basis on which people can live together in peace with one another in the 'spirit of brotherhood'. To promote this principle, the United Nations General Assembly proclaimed 1995 as the United Nations Year for Tolerance. It noted that 'tolerance – the recognition and appreciation of others, the ability to live together with and to listen to others – is the sound foundation of any civil society and of peace'.[142] UNESCO, at whose initiative the Year was proclaimed, was invited to assume the role of lead organization. The UNESCO instrument 'Declaration of Principles on Tolerance (1995)' further promoted this principle.

The 2005 World Summit outlined the commitment of the UN Member States to encourage tolerance, respect, dialogue and cooperation among different cultures, civilizations and peoples (World Summit Outcome Document, General Assembly Resolution 60/1, 24 October 2005, para. 145).

Article 2.

Everyone is entitled to all the rights and freedoms set forth in this Declaration, without distinction of any kind, such as race, colour, sex, language, religion, political or other opinion, national or social origin, property, birth or other status. Furthermore, no distinction shall be made on the basis of the political, jurisdictional or international status of the country or territory to which a person belongs, whether it be independent, trust, non-self-governing or under any other limitation of sovereignty.

Article 7.

All are equal before the law and are entitled without any discrimination to equal protection of the law. All are entitled to equal protection against any discrimination in violation of this Declaration and against any incitement to such discrimination.

These two Articles express the guiding principle of the Declaration and all subsequent human rights instruments of non-discrimination. It constitutes a crucial principle in the protection of human rights. Article 2 concerns non-discrimination in application of the provisions of the Declaration, whereas Article 7 ensures non-discrimination in the application of the law in general, that is, essentially, national laws. Article 7 demands that all States ensure that no distinction of any kind is made in their legal systems in respect of any of the criteria established by Article 2. Equal protection before the law also binds law enforcement officials, e.g. the judiciary and the police, and demands a system in which everyone has access to legal defence. Furthermore, States have a duty to protect all minorities against any form of discrimination. It also means that it is illegal to 'incite' such discrimination, that is, to encourage others to practise discrimination.

The Human Rights Committee (see Part I, Questions 14–17), in its interpretation of the corresponding Article of the International Covenant on Civil and Political Rights, pointed out that the enjoyment of rights and freedoms on an equal footing does not mean identical treatment in every instance, for example, juvenile offenders should be segregated from adults. The Committee also pointed out that States Parties are required to employ affirmative action in order to diminish or eliminate conditions which cause or help to perpetuate discrimination prohibited by the Covenant (General Comment No. 18).

The International Convention on the Elimination of All Forms of Racial Discrimination (see Part I, Questions 31–33) defines racial discrimination as 'any distinction, exclusion, restriction or preference based on race, colour, descent, or national or ethnic origin which has the purpose or effect of nullifying or impairing the recognition, enjoyment or exercise, on an equal footing, of human rights and fundamental freedoms in the political, economic, social, cultural or any other field of public life' (Article 1).

The practice of racism and racial discrimination stems primarily from notions of superiority and inferiority of racial or ethnic groups, which are used to justify the servitude and even the elimination of 'lesser' beings. Any such theory, according to UNESCO's Declaration on Race and Racial Prejudice, adopted in 1978, 'has no scientific foundation and is contrary to the moral and ethical principles of humanity' (Article 2, para. 1).

How persistent are practices of racism and racial discrimination?

Discrimination on the grounds of racial or ethnic origin continues to be a major problem of our time and is manifested in a variety of ways. In the first half of the past century, humanity witnessed the effects of anti-Semitic racist theories, culminating in the Nazis' attempt to eliminate the Jews, and other crimes against humanity carried out by totalitarian regimes.

Towards the close of the past century, humanity witnessed 'ethnic cleansing' in the former Yugoslavia, and the systematic mass killing in Rwanda. These are only two of the many recent instances of brutality committed in the course of ethnic or racial conflicts in all continents.

In earlier centuries, as part of colonial and imperial expansion, many powerful nations practised harmful policies of racial superiority and discrimination towards subject peoples. These sentiments are recurring in new manifestations of racism and xenophobia within European States. Millions of migrant workers, refugees and displaced persons, and other non-nationals, as well as persons belonging to national or ethnic, religious and linguistic minorities living in Europe and in some other continents, are experiencing discriminatory attitudes, prejudicial violence and exploitation. Right-wing extremist political groups are on the rise, propagating militant racism and extreme nationalism.

In former colonial countries, many of the discriminatory practices and legacies of the past have become entrenched in patterns of discrimination and help to perpetuate ruling political, economic and social structures. Erstwhile victims of racial practices have themselves allowed racist doctrines to obscure their former quest for freedom.

South Africa represents a unique example of the dismantling of a statutory system of racial discrimination, and the subsequent bloodless transfer of political power. The system of apartheid, with its institutionalized separation of races as a particular form of racism and racial discrimination, existed for almost fifty years in South Africa. The first step towards a democratic society was taken in February 1990, when President de Klerk announced the unbanning of the proscribed political parties, followed by the release of Nelson Mandela after twenty-seven years of imprisonment, and the repeal of apartheid legislation. In 1991, a forum representing eighteen political organizations, including the then South African Government, was set up to prepare a post-apartheid political blueprint for the country. The following year a whites-only referendum agreed to abolish apartheid, thus endorsing equal political participation for all South Africans in the democratic process. In April 1994, a multi-party election based on universal suffrage took place, resulting in the establishment of a five-year interim Government of National Unity, headed by President Nelson Mandela, who stepped down in 1998. International organizations, in particular the United Nations system, played a major role in the elimination of apartheid.

In 2001, the International Year of Mobilization against Racism, Racial Discrimination, Xenophobia and Related Intolerance was proclaimed. The World Conference against Racism, Racial Discrimination, Xenophobia and Related Intolerance (Durban, 31 August–7 September 2001) adopted the Durban Declaration and Programme of Action to guide the struggle against discrimination and promote tolerance. The Durban Review Conference in April 2009 called for the implementation of the Durban Declaration and Programme of Action (see Question 35).

Article 3.
Everyone has the right to life, liberty and security of person.

Is it the responsibility of the State to ensure these rights?

Even though the protection of these rights is the duty of the State, they are persistently violated by some governments in many parts of

the world. There is extensive evidence, over recent years, of deaths in detention, as well as unaccounted disappearances of people.

The United Nations now reports regularly on enforced or involuntary disappearances, and arbitrary and extra-judicial executions in many countries of the world. The adoption of the Convention for the Protection of All Persons from Enforced Disappearance in 2006 and the creation of a monitoring Committee envisaged by the Convention, will further contribute to the system of protection from enforced disappearance (see Part I, Question 30). There is no evidence that the overall number of people victimized by these phenomena is decreasing. Together with torture, these constitute grave violations of human rights, demanding the constant attention of the world community.

In some cases the violation of the right to life goes as far as killing or physically or mentally harming with intent to destroy, wholly or in part, a national, ethnic, racial or religious group. Such acts are called genocide and represent an international crime, as stated in the International Convention on the Prevention and Punishment of the Crime of Genocide (see Part I, Question 25).

What if the laws of a State allow for the taking of human life through capital punishment?

Capital punishment exists in many countries, based on the widespread belief that the death penalty is a just punishment for the taking of a life and that it acts as a deterrent to others to commit similar crimes. There is no substantial evidence to support the belief that the death penalty has a deterrent effect. If the death penalty is carried out and subsequent findings reveal there was a miscarriage of justice, it is too late. There are many examples of innocent persons being executed even after the most rigorous of trials.

Public opinion for or against capital punishment changes with circumstances. People sometimes oppose the death penalty when innocent people have lost their lives, after a miscarriage of justice, or as a result of the excesses of a repressive regime, while a single sordid crime or the occurrence of 'new' crimes, like hijacking, political terrorism or kidnapping, can sway opinion the opposite

way. Opinion about the death penalty is influenced strongly by emotional factors. States also make laws to meet their momentary needs. 'States of Emergency' and 'States of Siege' often include provision for the death penalty to be instituted and based on the judgements by military tribunals or even by order of the government. The Commission on Human Rights prepared a study on the risks of such legislation for human rights.

The death penalty is, and often has been, used by repressive regimes as a tool of oppression against any opposition, and as an instrument for sustaining social injustice and racist policies.

Are there any international instruments aimed at the abolition of the death penalty?

This issue is an international human rights concern and both international and regional instruments have been created for its abolition. These are: the Second Optional Protocol to the International Covenant on Civil and Political Rights (1989); the Protocol to the American Convention on Human Rights, adopted by the Organization of American States (1990);[143] and Protocol No. 6 to the European Convention on Human Rights, adopted by the Council of Europe in 1983, and which entered into force in 1985.[144] These instruments are applicable to all States that have ratified them.

Article 4.
No one shall be held in slavery or servitude; slavery and the slave trade shall be prohibited in all their forms.

What does slavery mean today?

Today's slavery is not the brutal practice historically associated with the capture of humans, bound in chains, and sold on the open market. That type of slave trade has long since been abolished and the practice of slavery is outlawed in every country of the world, although vestiges of chattel slavery are still occasionally encountered. Nevertheless, many millions of people continue to live

in a state of servitude, mirroring in essence the same exploitation of one human being by another, in many countries of the world. Contemporary slavery remains a callous negation of human rights and dignity. Deeply rooted in economic and social structures, poverty, discrimination, ignorance, tradition and greed, these practices are extremely difficult to eradicate.

Such institutions and practices, similar to slavery but called by other names, are insidious and affect the weakest and most deprived strata of society. The Supplementary Convention on the Abolition of Slavery, the Slave Trade and Institutions and Practices Similar to Slavery (1956)[145] defines such institutions and practices as debt bondage, serfdom, exploitation of child labour and servile forms of marriage. Debt bondage is a condition arising from an exchange of personal service for debt, and the redemption of the debt thereby. It takes many forms and often operates in ways that hide the exploitative nature of the relationship. Found in many parts of the world, it is associated mainly with agriculture and migrant labour, and in many cases is institutionalized, thus ensuring a servile and defenceless labour force. In its worse form, when the debt is not redeemed, it can result in permanent servitude inherited by child from parent. In some situations, where peasants have tried to rebel against this practice, they have been violently repressed. At the root of this problem is the need for land reform. However, in some countries where legislation and land reform that should help to abolish this practice have been passed, there continues to be reluctance on the part of governments to ensure enforcement.

The exploitation of child labour is a worldwide problem. Work conditions are often hazardous and remuneration minimal or non-existent. Millions of children are, for the most part, deprived of education and subjected to conditions detrimental to their physical and mental welfare.

The ILO, according to the 2006 Global Report on Child Labour ('The end of Child Labour: Within Reach'), identifies the worst forms of child labour as involving 218 million children worldwide. Of those children, 126 million are in hazardous work and over 8 million are in the absolute worst forms of child labour, which are defined as slavery, trafficking, debt bondage, forced recruitment for use in armed conflict, pornography and illicit activities. The latter situations are addressed by ILO Convention No. 182 (1999), which

calls for immediate action to combat these forms of child labour, together with measures for their elimination and prevention in the longer term. An earlier ILO Convention, No. 38 (1973), provides a comprehensive framework with respect to the minimum age for employment. The inclusion of a clause calling for the effective abolition of child labour in the ILO Declaration on Fundamental Principles and Rights at Work and its follow-up (see Part I, Question 82) emphasizes the consensus on the seriousness of the issue.

Measures to address other aspects of the exploitation of child labour can be found in the two Protocols to the Convention on the Rights of the Child (See Part I, Questions 44–45).

Women are also among those particularly affected by such practices. Servile marriages result from situations where women, with no right to refuse, are given in marriage in exchange for payment of money or kind; or are transferred by the husband or family to another person for value received; or are inherited 'upon the death of her husband' by another person. Another slavery-like practice, particularly affecting women and children, is that of traffic in persons. This is covered by the Convention on the Suppression of the Traffic in Persons and of the Exploitation of the Prostitution of Others (1949), which, at the time of writing, had only been ratified by 81 countries.[146]

What can be done to eradicate slavery in all its forms?

Slavery and slavery-like practices constitute a very complex problem, which is aggravated by the fact that many people deny its existence. The United Nations received information about such situations through evidence submitted to the Working Group on Slavery (appointed by the Sub-Commission on Human Rights) as well as information relating to the Convention for the Suppression of Trafficking in Persons and Exploitation of the Prostitution of Others. In 2007, the Human Rights Council decided to replace the Working Group on Slavery by the Special Rapporteur on Contemporary Forms of Slavery, including its Causes and Consequences. More than 120 States have ratified the Supplementary Convention on the Abolition of Slavery. Adherence ultimately depends upon implementation at the national level. However, no international

mechanism exists to monitor and enforce States' obligations to abolish slavery and related practices. Significant progress towards the eradication of these practices will depend upon political will, widespread education, social reform and economic development.

Article 5.
No one shall be subjected to torture or to cruel, inhuman or degrading treatment or punishment.

What is meant by torture?

The Convention against Torture and Other Cruel, Inhuman or Degrading Treatment or Punishment, which was adopted by consensus on 10 December 1984 by the United Nations General Assembly (see Part I, Questions 26–27), defines torture as 'any act by which severe pain or suffering, whether physical or mental, is intentionally inflicted on a person for such purposes as obtaining from him or a third person information or a confession, punishing him for an act he or a third person has committed or is suspected of having committed, or intimidating or coercing him or a third person, or for any reason based on discrimination of any kind, when such pain or suffering is inflicted by or at the instigation of or with the consent or acquiescence of a public official or other person acting in an official capacity. It does not include pain or suffering arising only from, inherent in or incidental to lawful sanctions' (Article 1). The Vienna Declaration and Programme of Action (1993) emphasized that 'one of the most atrocious violations against human dignity is the act of torture, the result of which destroys the dignity and impairs the capability of victims to continue their lives and their activities' (II, para. 55).

What is meant by cruel, inhuman or degrading treatment or punishment?

The most widely accepted interpretation of these terms is contained in Article 6 of the 'Body of Principles for the Protection of All Persons under Any Form of Detention or Imprisonment' (see Part I,

Question 59). It is intended to 'extend the widest protection against abuses, whether physical or mental including the holding of a detained or imprisoned person in conditions which deprive her, temporarily or permanently, of the use of any natural senses such as sight or hearing, or of his awareness of place and passing of time'.

Where is torture practised, why is it practised and who are the torturers?

Torture knows no geographical boundaries, nor can it be ascribed to a single political ideology or to one economic system. Many non-governmental organizations have substantiated thousands of documented cases of torture from all parts of the world.

Torture today is not merely the occasional lapse of legal restraints in a few isolated incidents; rather, it reflects a conscious choice of the highest governmental officials to destroy the legal restraints that would inhibit the excesses of that power. Some governments (and some insurgency movements) use torture as a means of gaining information, of forcing confessions, and of terrorizing the general population. When a person is held in incommunicado detention, in other words, without access to a lawyer, family and relatives or groups belonging to civil society, torture frequently occurs.

Can torture be justified?

No, neither morally nor legally. Most national legal systems as well as international law explicitly forbid the use of torture. All Member States of the United Nations are required to respect Article 5 of the Universal Declaration of Human Rights, which prohibits torture. Some will argue that, under exceptional circumstances, the use of torture is justified. Should not the State use every means available, they will ask, to obtain information from a terrorist who has put innocent lives in danger? Apart from the clear moral and legal principles that forbid torture categorically, the argument for torture is misguided on several grounds: first, torture can produce false confessions and erroneous information; second, torture offends the

principle of just punishment; third, the use of torture in a single case creates a precedent for its use on a much broader scale and at the discretion of the State.

What can be done to stop torture?

The granting of full legal rights to a detainee is the obvious means of preventing torture. An independent judiciary and adequate access by the detainee to legal and medical counsel of his or her choice are essential. At the international level, publicity about torture and interventions by governments and by intergovernmental and non-governmental organizations on behalf of individuals in danger of torture can help to ensure that the national legal system offers adequate protection to a particular person. Codes of ethics and conduct have been established to both guide and protect the law-enforcement officers, lawyers or medical personnel who most frequently come into contact with the victims of torture and upon whose courage may depend on the exposure of torture cases.

Article 6.
Everyone has the right to recognition everywhere as a person before the law.

Article 7.
This Article is considered together with Article 2 above.

Article 8.
Everyone has the right to an effective remedy by the competent national tribunals for acts violating the fundamental rights granted him by the constitution or by law.

Article 6 is the first in a series of Articles that cover the more 'legalistic' human rights. The phrase 'person before the law' refers to the recognition that States should give to the right of all individuals to make, for example, agreements or contracts that courts will enforce, and start proceedings before courts to ensure that their legal rights are enforced.

A very important part of these Articles is the word 'everyone'. It indicates that no difference or distinction may be made by a State between any of its own citizens, foreigners or stateless persons in the enforcement of all the rights which a 'person before the law' possesses.

What can a person do when his or her constitutional or legal rights are violated?

The aim of Article 8 is to create a right of recourse to a domestic tribunal or a court for a person who feels that his or her constitutional or legal rights have been violated. It does not relate

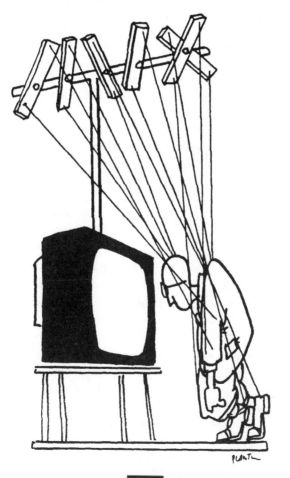

to rights contained in the Universal Declaration, but only to those rights that are guaranteed by the constitution or laws of a State itself.

It means that no situation should ever arise where a person is without a remedy when his or her legal rights are violated. Further, the fact that 'everyone' is specifically mentioned means that the right to a remedy (for example, the right to sue) may not be restricted to certain groups of people. The word 'competent' refers to courts that have been designated for a certain purpose (thus a person who claims that his or her industrial rights have been violated should petition to a court specialized in this question and not to a court which deals, say, with family law).

Article 9.
No one shall be subjected to arbitrary arrest, detention or exile.

Can such treatment ever be justified?

This Article is the first of three Articles which deal with the fundamental legal safeguards that all legal systems should ensure to individuals: freedom from arbitrary arrest, the right to a fair and prompt trial and the presumption of innocence. The meaning of Article 9 is self-evident except, perhaps, for the term 'arbitrary'. Two possible interpretations of it are frequently advanced: one is that persons may only be arrested, detained or exiled in accordance with legal procedures; the other is that nobody should be subjected to arrest, detention or exile of a capricious or random character, where there is no likelihood that he or she committed an offence.

The first interpretation seems inadequate, as laws often allow sweeping powers of arrest and because legal procedures may often themselves be arbitrary or abused. The protection thus offered by such an interpretation is not adequate to meeting such threats to human dignity. The second interpretation is therefore the only valid one. It is particularly so due to the fact that arbitrary, albeit procedurally legal, arrest often may be followed by the wrongful treatment or torture of a detainee (see also Part I, Questions 26–29).

Article 10.

Everyone is entitled in full equality to a fair and public hearing by an independent and impartial tribunal, in the determination of his rights and obligations and of any criminal charge against him.

Article 10 provides for the basic right to a fair trial. It refers not only to criminal cases but also to civil disputes where one person sues another. The purpose of the Article is to guarantee a fair hearing, by an independent and impartial tribunal, to all those who appear in court.

Although it is sometimes argued that notions of 'fair', 'independent' and 'impartial' differ from country to country, it is clear that everybody must have a fair chance to state his or her case. The Basic Principles on the Independence of the Judiciary[147] are expected to be taken into account by States.

Article 11.

(1) Everyone charged with a penal offence has the right to be presumed innocent until proved guilty according to law in a public trial at which he has had all the guarantees necessary for his defence.
(2) No one shall be held guilty of any penal offence on account of any act or omission which did not constitute a penal offence, under national or international law, at the time when it was committed. Nor shall a heavier penalty be imposed than the one that was applicable at the time the penal offence was committed.

Article 11 covers four basic principles:
The presumption of innocence. This is a simple but important concept. It means that anyone who is charged with a criminal offence should not be treated as being guilty until his or her guilt has been proved. In some countries, it is the basis of the right to have bail, which means that an accused person may retain his or her liberty pending trial.
The right to a defence. The word 'guarantee' in Article 11 includes, for example, the obligation of a State to ensure that an accused person has both legal representation and proper possibilities to establish his or her innocence, including the right to call witnesses.

The right to a public hearing. The maxim 'justice should not only be done but should be seen to be done' is implicit here. To ensure confidence in the law, it is necessary to give people the possibility to see that the law is applied openly, and to witness how legal machinery works in practice. If trials are held in secret, there is no guarantee that fundamental rights are being respected. This part of

Article 11 imposes a duty on States to show that the law is being fairly and properly applied.

Non-retroactivity of law. This cumbersome phrase involves a very simple idea. A person shall not be punished for those acts that were legal when they were committed. It also means that, if an act was punishable in one way when committed, a later change in the law may not increase the punishment given.

The inclusion of 'international law' in paragraph 2 of this Article is a reference to, in particular, the Nuremberg and Tokyo trials of the major war criminals, which took place at the end of the Second World War. War crimes and crimes against humanity were tried before international tribunals on the basis of laws of worldwide applicability (international law) rather than the specific laws of States.

Article 12.

No one shall be subjected to arbitrary interference with his privacy, family, home or correspondence, nor to attacks upon his honour and reputation. Everyone has the right to the protection of the law against such interference or attacks.

Domestic laws vary as do customs and cultures. The legal interpretations and limitations imposed by governments or local laws and traditions are equally varied when it comes to 'privacy', 'family', 'home', 'honour' and 'reputation'. The implementation of this right is therefore eventually to be found in national legislation. Particular problems arise as a result of modern electronic technologies, such as illicit access to confidential information in data banks or the practice of 'wiretapping' private telephone conversations. Abuses are all the more difficult to detect and prove.

However, in a number of countries legislation exists to protect these fundamental freedoms, and non-governmental organizations and the media take issue against their violation.

Article 13.

(1) Everyone has the right to freedom of movement and residence within the borders of each State.
(2) Everyone has the right to leave any country, including his own, and to return to his country.

Article 12 of the International Covenant on Civil and Political Rights elaborates further this right and adds that the only possible restrictions are those 'which are provided by law, are necessary to protect public security, public order *(ordre public)*, public health or morals, or the rights and freedoms of others, and are consistent with the other rights recognized in the present Covenant'. These rights, according to Article 4 of the same Covenant, may be suspended 'in time of public emergency which threatens the life of the nation and the existence of which is officially proclaimed' (see Part I, Question 13). These exceptions should be of a temporary nature and based on the legitimate need to protect the safety of others. Thus a natural disaster, epidemic or war would necessitate certain restrictions on this right. Other restrictions may be made in order to prevent someone with charges pending under the domestic laws from leaving his/her country; similarly those in prison would have to serve their sentences before being free to leave the country. None of these exceptions implies, however, the acceptance of any form of arbitrary or permanent restriction of this right.

In which ways can freedom of movement be restricted?

There are many ways in which freedom of movement, both within and between countries, is restricted by governments. Some governments, for political reasons, restrict internal movement of their own citizens, as well as that of foreigners. Arbitrary detention (see Article 9, above) continues to be practised, and labour camps persist as a means of confining citizens because of their political opposition or dissent. Such practices are hidden when governments claim spurious legitimate reasons to justify these illegitimate practices.

In times of internal strife and/or armed conflict, extensive internal displacements of people as well as massive exoduses occur, all of which are, by and large, coerced movements, with no guarantee of the right of individuals to return to their homes, thus constituting a denial of the principle of freedom of movement. Sadly, there are all too many examples of these occurrences, which stem, in the first instance, from gross violations of basic human rights and fundamental freedoms.

Article 14.
(1) Everyone has the right to seek and to enjoy in other countries asylum from persecution.
(2) This right may not be invoked in the case of prosecutions genuinely arising from non-political crimes or from acts contrary to the purposes and principles of the United Nations.

What is meant by asylum?

Asylum implies the provision of refuge and protection for persons who have left their own country for fear of being persecuted (see Part I, Question 54).

The 1951 UN Refugee Convention provides protection against persecution. However, neither persecution nor the characteristics of the perpetrators of persecution are defined. The view held by the UNHCR is that the Convention applies to any person who has a well-founded fear of persecution, regardless of who the perpetrator is. While this view is shared by a majority of States, others do not recognize 'fear of persecution', where persecution is attributed to non-state actors. But the reality is that persecution stems from far wider sources than States or even unofficial armed groups. Traditional customs, clans, sects or families may be the basis of persecution. Thus the protection of the Convention may extend to women in vulnerable situations, who may have transgressed the social mores of a society, and for whom the State has failed to provide protection. For these women, becoming a refugee is the only means of escape. In the industrialized countries, the preservation of asylum is a major issue. Legal provisions governing asylum are built around the control of unregulated migration, such as outflows of people from war-torn areas and the increasing phenomenon of trafficking and smuggling of people. This has led to tighter controls and to the blurring of the distinction between refugees and economic migrants.

While granting asylum remains a prerogative of the State to exercise at its discretion, most States are committed to preserving the right to seek asylum and thus accept the challenge to ensure respect of basic human rights principles in the exercise of their prerogative.

Article 15.
(1) Everyone has the right to a nationality.
(2) No one shall be arbitrarily deprived of his nationality nor denied the right to change his nationality.

Why do people need a nationality?

Nationality is one of the attributes necessary both for the material as well as the spiritual well-being of persons within society. Nationality provides the individual with an identity. In a material sense, this identity is related to a geographic location and the implicit entitlement to the protection of the laws in operation within the jurisdiction of the State. The State also has responsibilities for the protection of its nationals on the territory of other States. In terms of identity, a nationality provides the individual with a sense of belonging and a sense of self-worth. Article 24 of the International Covenant on Civil and Political Rights explicitly provides for the right of every child to acquire a nationality while Article 8 of the Convention on the Rights of the Child requires the State to 'respect the right of the child to preserve his or her identity, including nationality [...] without unlawful interference'.

What protection is there for people deprived of their nationality?

Political controversy and conflicts often surround the whole question of nationality. In recent times, ethno-nationalism has been a significant factor in many violent conflicts. The emergence of new States has sometimes gone hand in hand with persecution, and expulsion of people, and the escalation of statelessness. Minorities, who form a significant sector of the contemporary refugee population, are particularly affected.

The Convention on the Reduction of Statelessness (1961)[148] seeks to oblige a State to provide a nationality for anyone born in its territory, who would otherwise be stateless, and to prohibit the withdrawal of nationality from a person who would thereby be made

stateless. Under no circumstances may a person be deprived of his or her nationality on racial, ethnic, religious or political grounds.

Article 16.
(1) Men and women of full age, without any limitation due to race, nationality or religion, have the right to marry and to found a family. They are entitled to equal rights as to marriage, during marriage and at its dissolution.
(2) Marriage shall be entered into only with the free and full consent of the intending spouses.
(3) The family is the natural and fundamental group unit of society and is entitled to protection by society and the State.

Attitudes with respect to marriage differ and family laws are often based on religious, cultural and social patterns. The notion of 'free and full consent' raises special problems for certain cultures and the rules relating to this matter have been set out in greater detail in the United Nations Convention on the Consent to Marriage, Minimum Age for Marriage and Registration of Marriages (1962)[149] and the Recommendation on the same subject adopted by the United Nations General Assembly in 1965.

The notion of family varies widely from that of the 'nuclear family', and indeed the single-parent family, to that of the extended family in many other parts of the world. Nevertheless, it does constitute a basic element in any society, and States have the obligation to protect it, as formulated in Article 10 of the International Covenant on Economic, Social and Cultural Rights and Article 23 of the International Covenant on Civil and Political Rights.

Article 17.
(1) Everyone has the right to own property alone as well as in association with others.
(2) No one shall be arbitrarily deprived of his property.

Property was placed on the same level as freedom, security and resistance against oppression in the French Declaration of the Rights of Man and of the Citizen (1789). After over 200 years of social and

economic history, the concept of ownership in relation to human rights has evolved and is still a complex and controversial matter. Due to the ideological confrontation that prevailed at the time of the adoption of the International Covenants, the right to property is the only one mentioned in the Universal Declaration of Human Rights that was not included in the Covenants. However, any discrimination concerning the right to own property, as well as the protection of intellectual property, falls clearly within international human rights law.

Article 18.
Everyone has the right to freedom of thought, conscience and religion; this right includes freedom to change his religion or belief, and freedom, either alone or in community with others and in public or private, to manifest his religion or belief in teaching, practice, worship and observance.

Freedom of thought, conscience, religion and belief are fundamental freedoms, which may not be suspended, even in states of emergency.

The same protection is due to religious believers as to non-believers. No one may be discriminated against because of his/her religion and belief, nor forced to adhere to any other. This freedom to practise one's religion or belief (either alone or in community with others) encompasses a broad range of activities and customs (i.e. specific ceremonies, dietary regulations, distinctive clothing, freedom to establish religious schools and seminaries and to distribute religious texts and publications, and the right to have specific places of worship).

This freedom may be threatened by States whose attitude towards religion differs widely, ranging from encouraging all to adhere to an official religion to discouraging any religious belief. Protection should always be extended to freedom of thought as an individual right regardless of the beliefs of the prevailing majority or official attitudes. Despite controversial perceptions of this freedom, the international community's concern regarding intolerance and discrimination in these spheres is manifested in the adoption of the Declaration on the Elimination of All Forms of Intolerance and of Discrimination Based on Religion or Belief (United Nations General Assembly Resolution 36/55 of 25 November 1981).

To promote the implementation of this Declaration, a Special Rapporteur on Freedom of Religion or Belief was appointed by the Commission on Human Rights in 1986 (the initial mandate title was Special Rapporteur on Religious Intolerance, which was changed by the Commission in 2000). In his 2002 report to the Commission on Human Rights, the Rapporteur expressed deep concern at the continuing and escalating manifestations of religious intolerance and discrimination in numerous regions of the world. He underlined that religious extremism and instrumentalization of religion threaten the enjoyment of human rights, in general, and the right to peace in particular. In 2007, the Human Rights Council (replacing the Commission on Human Rights) renewed the Rapporteur's mandate for a period of 3 years.

The Commission on Human Rights recognized conscientious objection to military service as a legitimate exercise of the right to freedom of thought, conscience and religion (Resolution 1993/84). The Resolution appeals to States with compulsory military service to introduce alternative forms of public service for conscientious objectors.

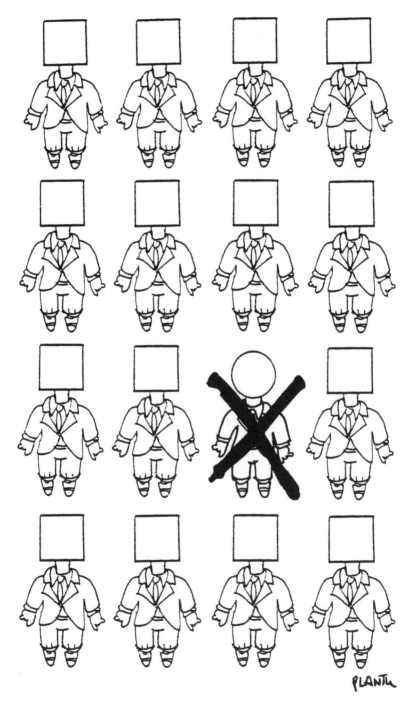

PLANTU

Article 19.
Everyone has the right to freedom of opinion and expression; this right includes freedom to hold opinions without interference and to seek, receive and impart information and ideas through any media and regardless of frontiers.

The protection and exercise of these rights are essential components of a democratic society (see also Article 21). The freedom to 'seek and impart information and ideas through any media' calls for the media to be free and independent, to criticize the government and to stimulate debate on policy.

The underlying motive behind repression of freedom of opinion and expression is fear: fear of the challenge presented by alternative views and fear that derives from the knowledge that freedom of opinion and expression is a basic tool for securing every other fundamental freedom. While governments do succeed in restricting these freedoms within their own jurisdiction, there is no way in which they can ultimately stifle free thought, opinion and expression. Banning books does not erase them, and prohibiting their publication does not preclude them from being published and read elsewhere, or from being circulated in another form. Modern technology is a very significant factor in promoting the flow of and access to information.

Are there any international safeguards for freedom of the media and of information?

The action of the United Nations and its specialized agencies has been mainly in support of professional bodies and non-governmental organizations that work actively in defence of freedom of expression and freedom of the media.

In 1989, UNESCO adopted a new Communication Strategy 'to encourage the free flow of information at international as well as national levels and its wider and better balanced dissemination without any obstacle to the freedom of expression'. Under this strategy, UNESCO organized regional seminars for media professionals in Eastern and Central Europe (Paris, 1989 and 1990); Africa (Windhoek, 1991); Asia (Almaty, 1992); Latin America and

the Caribbean (Santiago de Chile, 1994); and in the Arab States (1996). In March 2008, UNESCO held an Experts' Group Meeting in Paris regarding the Freedom of Information and Sustainable Development, thus underlining the important link between the access to information and development issues.

In countries undergoing transition to democratic structures, UNESCO actively assists in advising on media legislation. For countries in conflict, UNESCO supports independent media to promote non-partisan reporting and thereby contributes to creating an atmosphere for dialogue and peace.

A Special Rapporteur on the Promotion and Protection of the Right to Freedom of Opinion and Expression was appointed by the Commission on Human Rights in 1993, in order to make practical and action-oriented recommendations as to how these rights can be better protected. The Rapporteur's mandate was renewed by the Human Rights Council in 2008 for a period of three years.

The issues of freedom of expression and information have been considered on a number of occasions by the European Court of Human Rights and the Inter-American Court of Human Rights and their decisions have served the development of customary law in this sphere.

Are these freedoms absolute?

The International Covenant on Civil and Political Rights states that the exercise of freedom of opinion and expression 'carries with it special duties and responsibilities', and may thus be 'subject to certain restrictions but these shall be such as provided by law and are necessary for the respect of the rights and reputation of others, for the protection of national security or of public order or of public health or morals' (Article 19). The Covenant also prohibits 'any propaganda for war' or 'any advocacy of national, racial or religious hatred that constitutes incitement to discrimination, hostility or violence' (Article 20). Freedom of expression is therefore not absolute, but, in general terms, any restriction must meet the criteria of legitimacy, legality, proportionality and democratic necessity. Clear rules should protect the individual's reputation and privacy in relation to the media.

Article 20.
(1) Everyone has the right to freedom of peaceful assembly and association.
(2) No one may be compelled to belong to an association.

Freedom of association is the only way in which people can collectively express their aims, exercise pressure as a group and protect their own interests or the interests of others. No positive action by the government is required to ensure this freedom. On the other hand, governments may restrict it. Though there are some legitimate reasons why this might be done in certain circumstances, such restrictions are all too frequently exercised as a means of repression by States in many parts of the world.

The International Labour Organization has adopted several conventions on the particular right to association for workers which

have been ratified by a great number of countries.[150] The right to
freedom of association (ILO Convention No. 87) reflects one of
the eight fundamental principles in respect of workers' rights (see
Part I, Question 82).

Article 21.
(1) Everyone has the right to take part in the
government of his country, directly or through freely
chosen representatives.
(2) Everyone has the right of equal access to public
service in his country.
(3) The will of the people shall be the basis of the
authority of government; this will shall be expressed
in periodic and genuine elections which shall be by
universal and equal suffrage and shall be held by secret
vote or by equivalent free voting procedures.

This Article endorses the principles of democratic government in that 'the will of the people shall be the basis for the authority of government'. This is to be achieved through 'genuine elections', i.e. free and fair elections based on universal suffrage. While such elections are a crucial element in the process of democratization, protection of human rights and the rule of law constitute other integral requirements. The Montreal Plan of Action, which underlines that 'democratic values are required for the enjoyment of human rights', was the first internationally accepted document that recognized education for democracy as an integral part of education for human rights. The Vienna Declaration and Programme of Action (1993), reflecting global consensus, confirmed that the relationship between human rights, fundamental freedoms, and democracy, on the one hand, and development, on the other, is 'inter-dependent and mutually reinforcing' (Article 8). It called on the international community 'to support the strengthening and promotion of democracy' because the protection and promotion of human rights, fundamental freedoms and the rule of law is best achieved in all States through the application of democratic principles.

By its Resolution on Representative Democracy (1991), the Organization of American States (OAS) committed itself to holding a high-level political meeting within ten days of the interruption of the democratic process in any of its Member States. This Resolution underlines the recognition by the OAS of the intrinsic link between human rights and democracy.

Article 22.
Everyone, as a member of society, has the right to social security and is entitled to realization, through national effort and international co-operation and in accordance with the organization and resources of each State, of the economic, social and cultural rights indispensable for his dignity and the free development of his personality.

This Article, as well as Articles 23–27, deals with economic, social and cultural rights, which aim at the realization of both material and non-material human needs to ensure the full development of human potential. The implementation of these rights requires positive action on the part of the State and the international community to

ensure that these rights become a reality for all. The International Covenant on Economic, Social and Cultural Rights (see Part I, Questions 18–23) stipulates the right of everyone to social security (Article 9).

One fifth of the world's population is afflicted by poverty and hunger. Disease, illiteracy and social insecurity are ever-increasing phenomena. The massive denial of basic social, economic and cultural rights merits equal outrage, on the part of the international community, as that accorded to the denial of civil and political rights.

Moreover, democracy, stability and peace cannot be sound unless there is full recognition of the interdependence and inter-relatedness of economic, social, cultural, political and civil rights. Economic growth, while essential, is not sufficient in itself to ensure the general well-being of peoples. Its advantages do not inevitably benefit all strata of the population. Hence, national efforts and international cooperation to promote economic and social advancement should also be concerned with creating fairer conditions to ensure the maximization and equitable enjoyment of economic, social and cultural rights. In aspiring to these rights, each country

has to take into account its own resources and priorities and to make all efforts to achieve the standards prescribed.

The right to social security also means that a society is responsible for ensuring protective security for its vulnerable and disadvantaged members in order to prevent them from sinking into greater deprivation.

Article 23.
(1) Everyone has the right to work, to free choice of employment, to just and favourable conditions of work and to protection against unemployment.
(2) Everyone, without any discrimination, has the right to equal pay for equal work.
(3) Everyone who works has the right to just and favourable remuneration ensuring for himself and his family an existence worthy of human dignity, and supplemented, if necessary, by other means of social protection.
(4) Everyone has the right to form and to join trade unions for the protection of his interests.

What international provisions safeguard the conditions of work and the rights of working people?

The above provisions have been further codified (Articles 6, 7 and 8) by the International Covenant on Economic, Social and Cultural Rights (see Part I, Questions 18–23), and their implementation is followed up by the Committee on Economic, Social and Cultural Rights. The ILO (see Part I, Questions 78–83) has the special responsibility of protecting working people. Its supervisory bodies publish reports every year on the extent to which ILO Conventions are being respected, and the organization also provides practical help to promote and implement these rights.

Migrant workers are a particularly vulnerable category of workers, as they do not enjoy all the rights of citizens (see Part I, Question 52).

Article 24.
Everyone has the right to rest and leisure, including reasonable limitation of working hours and periodic holidays with pay.

Although organized labour has progressively obtained recognition of the limitation of working hours and conditions of work, it is still the fate of millions in the world to work without adequate human rights protection. Through the efforts of the ILO, limitations on the working week have gained international recognition. Doubts have been expressed about the status of rest and leisure as human rights, but this Article of the Universal Declaration of Human Rights, as well as Article 7 of the International Covenant on Economic, Social and Cultural Rights, make it very clear that they are included among universally recognized human rights.

Article 25.
(1) Everyone has the right to a standard of living adequate for the health and well-being of himself and of his family, including food, clothing, housing and medical care and necessary social services, and the right to security in the event of unemployment, sickness, disability, widowhood, old age or other lack of livelihood in circumstances beyond his control.
(2) Motherhood and childhood are entitled to special care and assistance. All children, whether born in or out of wedlock, shall enjoy the same social protection.

What is meant by the right to an adequate standard of living?

Different people would give different answers to this question. However, no one can deny that the very least it means is that every person is entitled to satisfy the basic human needs of food, shelter, clothing, household requirements and community services such as water, sanitation, health and education. It also means that everyone should have the right to work in order to achieve a decent

standard of living and that social security should be provided for those who cannot do so.

Those who are in greatest need should be given prior consideration and development objectives should give priority to the poorest, the most underprivileged and those who suffer deprivation through discrimination.

The right to an adequate standard of living is elaborated in Article 11 of the Covenant on Economic, Social and Cultural

Rights which stipulates specifically the fundamental right of everyone to be free from hunger and points to measures to be taken individually and through international cooperation towards the achievement of this right.

Article 26.
(1) Everyone has the right to education. Education shall be free, at least in the elementary and fundamental stages. Elementary education shall be compulsory. Technical and professional education shall be made generally available and higher education shall be equally accessible to all on the basis of merit.
(2) Education shall be directed to the full development of the human personality and to the strengthening of respect for human rights and fundamental freedoms. It shall promote understanding, tolerance and friendship among all nations, racial or religious groups, and shall further the activities of the United Nations for the maintenance of peace.
(3) Parents have a prior right to choose the kind of education that shall be given to their children.

Priorities of various countries in the field of education vary greatly. While compulsory education prevails in many countries, in a large part of the world universal literacy has not yet been achieved. A significant proportion of the world's adult population remains illiterate. The right to education is negated by the denial of equal access to education, which arises mainly because of deprivation, poverty, exclusion and discrimination.

Choices in education have to be relevant to the needs of a particular society, and the minimal requirement of free primary education is still a distant goal for many. Even where primary and secondary education are free and compulsory, educational choice and equal opportunities for education may be affected by the location of schools, imbalance in financing, libraries and equipment, or standards of teacher-training. The Commission on Human Rights appointed a Special Rapporteur on Education in 1998 to report on the progressive realization of this right throughout the world, and to make recommendations towards this end. The Rapporteur's

mandate was renewed by the Human Rights Council in 2008 (see Part I, Question 23).

Access to higher level and university education in most countries is not free. Provision of scholarships, extramural classes, adult education courses and on-the-job training are measures whereby further education can be promoted.

How is respect for human rights promoted through education?

The universally valid wider objective in education is the full development of the human personality and the strengthening of respect for human rights and fundamental freedoms. The Preamble to the Universal Declaration of Human Rights calls on 'every individual and every organ of society... [to] strive by teaching and education to promote respect for these rights and freedoms...'. In accordance with international human rights instruments, education should aim at the building of a universal culture of human rights through the imparting of knowledge and skills and the moulding of attitudes which are directed to:

(a) The strengthening of respect for human rights and fundamental freedoms.

(b) The full development of the human personality and the sense of its dignity.

(c) The promotion of understanding, tolerance, gender equality and friendship among all nations, indigenous peoples and racial, national, ethnic, religious and linguistic groups.

(d) The enabling of all persons to participate effectively in a free society.

(e) The furtherance of the activities of the United Nations for the maintenance of peace.

These aims should be promoted at all levels of formal education and non-formal learning, including preschool, primary and secondary school, higher education, professional schools, training of public officials and general public information. The United Nations agencies have adopted this approach in all activities relating to education and training. Since 2004, the United Nations have been promoting the World Programme on Human Rights Education in order to advance human rights education at all levels. On 10 December 2008, the International Year of Human rights Learning commenced (see Part I, Question 109).

UNESCO has developed these ideas in the Recommendation on Education for International Understanding, Co-operation and Peace and Education relating to Human Rights and Fundamental Freedoms (1974). Pursuant to this Recommendation, UNESCO's

Plan for the Development of Human Rights Teaching was elaborated in 1979 and has since been followed up in various ways. The UNESCO Strategy on Human Rights, adopted in 2003, identifies human rights education as one of the main UNESCO actions in this field (see Part I, Question 110).

Article 27.

(1) Everyone has the right freely to participate in the cultural life of the community, to enjoy the arts and to share in scientific advancement and its benefits.
(2) Everyone has the right to the protection of the moral and material interests resulting from any scientific, literary or artistic production of which he is the author.

UNESCO has elaborated specific provisions relating to this Article in the Recommendation concerning the Participation by the People at Large in Cultural Life and their Contribution to it (1976), the Recommendation on the Status of Scientific Researchers (1974) and various copyright conventions.

Cultural rights include the right of access to one's own culture and to the cultural heritage of others. Participation is an important aspect of the right to culture, which includes popular culture like drama, music, traditional dancing or carnivals. The right to culture also includes the right to benefit from scientific and technological progress. Broadly speaking, it also includes the right to education.

Cultural rights are still not as well codified as other categories of human rights and are often labelled as an 'underdeveloped' category of human rights.

Article 28.

Everyone is entitled to a social and international order in which the rights and freedoms set forth in this Declaration can be fully realized.

The very basic requirements for a life of dignity and minimal well-being are denied to a large proportion of mankind who live in conditions of great deprivation, poverty, hunger, disease and insecurity (see also Article 22). For such people, social justice is an

illusion as they are denied the conditions in which these rights and freedoms can be realized.

The way forward?

Despite several decades of international action devoted to development, the gap between rich and poor, at both international and national levels, continues to widen. This indicates that the maldistribution of the world's resources is reinforced by existing policies and institutions. Economic growth should not be an end in itself but a means towards meaningful development, based on the welfare of the human being.

Developing countries see themselves stifled by economic dependence and recognize that, in order to eliminate the inequalities, a new structure of international economic life is required, as well as relief from external debt burdens. Developed countries are slow to recognize that their own long-term interest in terms of peace, security and humanity lies in effecting change to the existing economic order by an act of political will.

The Vienna Declaration and Programme of Action (1993) reaffirmed the right to development as reflected in the Declaration on the Right to Development (see Part I, Question 115), and called for 'effective development policies at the national level, as well as equitable economic relations and a favourable economic environment at the international level'. The conclusions were confirmed and further elaborated by the World Summit for Social Development (Copenhagen, 6–12 March 1995).

The World Summit confirmed once again the principle of the universality, indivisibility, interrelatedness and interdependence of all human rights. Participating countries committed themselves to create an economic, political, social, cultural and legal environment that will enable people to achieve social development. They also committed themselves to the goal of eradicating poverty in the world through decisive national action and international cooperation and stressed the necessity to promote respect for democracy, the rule of law, pluralism and diversity, tolerance and responsibility, non-violence and solidarity.

In 1992, the Earth Summit in Rio de Janeiro adopted Agenda 21, a global plan of action for sustainable development, which integrated environmental, economic and social concerns in a single framework.

In December 2000, the United Nations General Assembly[151] called for a World Summit to regenerate, at the highest political level, the global commitment to sustainable development, a North-South partnership and accelerated action on Agenda 21, adopted in Rio.

The World Summit on Sustainable Development was held in Johannesburg, South Africa from 26 August to 4 September 2002 and adopted the Johannesburg Declaration on Sustainable Development and the Johannesburg Plan of Implementation. The Summit reaffirmed sustainable development as a central element of the international agenda and gave new impetus to global action to fight poverty and protect the environment. Support was gained for a world solidarity fund and for the eradication of poverty. In addition, a concept of partnership between governments, business and civil society was endorsed. The Summit also recognized the key role of civil society in implementing these outcomes and in promoting partnership initiatives. The subsequent draft resolution,[152] submitted to the General Assembly, reaffirmed the need to ensure a balance between economic development, social development and environmental protection as 'interdependent and mutually reinforcing pillars of sustainable development' and recognized that good governance within each country and at the international level is essential for this purpose.

The United Nation's Decade of Education for Sustainable Development, started in 2005, aims at mainstreaming sustainable development considerations in all aspects of education and training. As the lead UN agency of the Decade, UNESCO supports various initiatives related to the promotion of knowledge on sustainable development. Since autumn 2008 the global economic and financial crises have created additional obstacles to development and generated a negative impact on human rights.

Article 29.

(1) Everyone has duties to the community in which alone the free and full development of his personality is possible.

(2) In the exercise of his rights and freedoms, everyone shall be subject only to such limitations as are determined by law solely for the purpose of securing due recognition and respect for the rights and freedoms of others and of meeting the just requirements of morality, public order and the general welfare in a democratic society.

(3) These rights and freedoms may in no case be exercised contrary to the purposes and principles of the United Nations.

Is it justifiable to restrict freedom of political expression and organization in order to concentrate on the advancement of economic and social rights in areas of severe deprivation?

Many governments argue that they have conflicts of priorities with respect to the human rights enumerated in the Universal Declaration. There is no simple answer. While no direction of causality can be established between rights, there is an interdependence between civil and political rights and economic, social and cultural rights. The achievement of economic, social and cultural rights is indispensable to any form of social justice.

The Universal Declaration confirmed that freedom from fear and from want for all human beings can only be achieved if conditions are created whereby everyone can enjoy economic, social and cultural rights as well as civil and political rights.

The universality, indivisibility, interdependence and inter-relatedness of all human rights and fundamental freedoms was reaffirmed by the Vienna Declaration and Programme of Action (1993). It goes on to say: 'the international community must treat human rights globally and in a fair and equal manner, on the same footing, and with the same emphasis' (Article 5). The recognition

that all human rights are equally important in ensuring human dignity and freedom puts an end to lengthy and fruitless discussions on the priority of one or another category of rights.

What kind of duties does the individual have?

The Declaration asserts that it is only in the community that everyone can fully and freely develop his or her personality. It is therefore the duty of all persons in the community to uphold and claim their rights and freedoms, and respect those of others, in order to create the conditions within the community that make the full enjoyment of these rights and freedoms possible. Implicit too in the reference to 'everyone' is the recognition of the uniqueness of each individual human being which is the basis of the notion of human rights.

The second paragraph of Article 29 establishes a general rule concerning the limitations the State may place on the exercise of human rights in the collective interest. Nothing justifies the State placing undue restrictions on the exercise of the rights contained in the Universal Declaration of Human Rights. The laws of a democratic society should provide the framework within which rights and freedoms can thus be exercised. Moreover, it is the duty of the courts and the legitimate concern of everyone to ensure that any limitations placed by law upon the exercise of these rights and freedoms are used solely for a valid, recognized and just purpose.

What protection is there for individuals and groups who work to secure the promotion and respect of human rights?

The recognition of the vulnerability of such individuals and groups in some societies led to the adoption of the 'Declaration on the Right and Responsibility of Individuals, Groups and Organs of Society to protect Universally Recognized Human Rights and Fundamental Freedoms' by the General Assembly in 1998.

In essence, the Declaration is intended to be a blueprint for the protection of human rights defenders, who, in many parts of the world, and at risk to themselves, seek to promote and protect universally recognized human rights standards (see Part I, Question 60).

Article 30.
Nothing in this Declaration may be interpreted as implying for any State, group or person any right to engage in any activity or to perform any act aimed at the destruction of any of the rights and freedoms set forth herein.

This means that the provisions of the Declaration must be implemented in good faith, so as not to undermine its very purpose. In no circumstances should it be used as a pretext for violating human rights. This rule applies not only to States, but also to groups and individuals. Thus, no one may take an Article of the Declaration out of context and apply it in such a way that other Articles would be violated. This concluding Article, as does the whole Declaration, requires constant vigilance and the courage to stand up for one's own rights and the rights of others. This vigilance and courage are the price we must all pay so that some day human rights will apply to all members of the human family in practice as well as in theory.

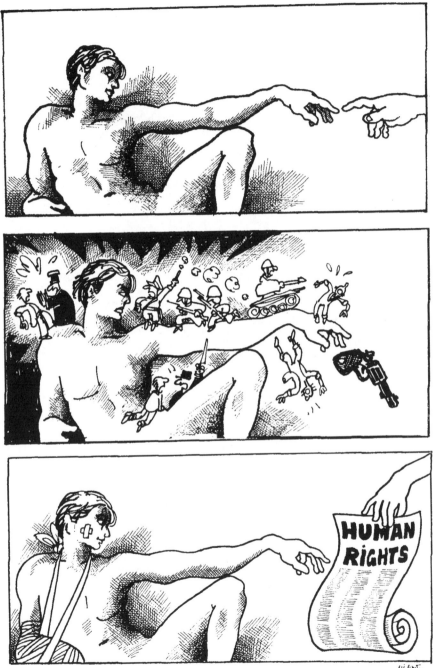

Endnotes

1   ILO Global Employment Trends Report 2009, p. 19, January 2009. Available at www.ilo.org/wcmsp5/groups/public/---dgreports/---dcomm/documents/publication/wcms_101461.pdf.

2   For more information visit Cartooning for Peace website: www.cartooningforpeace.org/.

3   Two important publications which examine the contributions of various streams of thought on human rights are: *Human Rights, Comments and Interpretations*, UNESCO (ed.), London/New York, Alban Wingate, 1948; and *Birthright of Man*, Jeanne Hersch (ed.), Paris, UNESCO, 1969.

4   Henri Dunant (1828–1910, Switzerland), the founder of the Red Cross, was, together with Frédéric Passy (France), the first Nobel Peace Prize Winner (1901).

5   General Assembly Resolution 60/1, 24 October 2005, World Summit Outcome Document.

6   Adopted by forty-eight votes with eight abstentions and no vote against.

7   General Assembly Resolution A/Res/63/117, 10 December 2008.

8   General Assembly Resolution 60/1, 24 October 2005, World Summit Outcome Document.

9   As at 31 May 2009, there were 192 Member States of the United Nations.

10   Proclamation of Tehran, adopted at the International Conference on Human Rights on 13 May 1968, para. 2.

11   The Vienna Declaration and Programme of Action, adopted on 25 June 1993 by the World Conference on Human Rights, Preamble, para. 8.

12   Ibid., operative part, para. 5.

13   A/Res/55/2.

14   As at 31 May 2009, 160 States had ratified the ICESCR. 164 States had ratified the ICCPR. For the names of States Parties, see *Human Rights Major International Instruments, Status as at 31 May 2009* (available at www.unesco.org/human_rights/ or www.unhchr.ch).

15   As at May 2009, 111 States had ratified the Optional Protocol to the ICCPR. For the list of States Parties, see *Human Rights Major International Instruments, Status as at 31 May 2009* (available at www.unesco.org/human_rights/ or www.unhchr.ch).

16   As at May 2009, 71 States had ratified the Second Optional Protocol to the International Covenant on Civil and Political Rights Aiming at the Abolition of the Death Penalty.
For the names of States Parties, see *Human Rights Major International Instruments, Status as at 31 January 2009* (available at www.unesco.org/human_rights/ or www.unhchr.ch).

17   As at 31 May 2009, the Optional Protocol to the International Covenant on Economic, Social and Cultural Rights had not yet in force. It will be open for signature in September 2009. See www.unhchr.ch.

18   Human Rights Committee, General Comment No 33, 'The Obligations of States Parties under the Optional Protocol to the International Covenent on Civil and Political Rights, 5 November 2008.

19   As at 31 May 2009, 140 States were Parties to the Convention on the Prevention and Punishment of the Crime of Genocide. For the list of States Parties, see *Human Rights Major International Instruments, Status as at 31 May 2009* (available at www.unesco.org/human_rights/ or www.unhchr.ch).

20   As at 31 May 2009, there were 146 States Parties to the Convention against Torture and Other Cruel, Inhuman or Degrading Treatment or Punishment. On this subject, see Nigel Rodley, *The Treatment of Prisoners under International Law*, Paris/Oxford, Unesco/Oxford University Press, 1987. It is also worth noting that the United Nations Voluntary Fund for Victims of Torture was established in 1981. For the list of States Parties, see *Human Rights Major International Instruments, Status as at 31 May 2009* (available at www.unesco.org/human_rights/ or www. unhchr.ch).

21   For the list of States Parties, see *Human Rights Major International Instruments, Status as at 31 May 2009* (available at www.unesco.org/human_rights/ or www. unhchr.ch).

22   As at 31 January 2009, 47 States had ratified the Optional Protocol to the Convention against Torture and Other Cruel, Inhuman or Degrading Treatment or Punishment, adopted in 2002. For the list of States Parties, see *Human Rights Major International Instruments, Status as at 31 May 2009* (available at www. unesco.org/human_rights/ or www.unhchr.ch).

23   As at 31 May 2009, all 47 States of the Council of Europe were parties to the European Convention for the Prevention of Torture and Inhuman or Degrading Treatment or Punishment. For the list of States Parties, see *Human Rights Major International Instruments, Status as at 31 May 2009* (available at www.unesco. org/human_rights/).

24   As at 31 May 2009, there were 17 parties to the Inter-American Convention to Prevent and Punish Torture. For the list of States Parties, see *Human Rights Major International Instruments, Status as at 31 May 2009* (available at www.unesco. org/human_rights/).

25   As at 31 May 2009, 10 States had ratified the International Convention for the protection of all Persons from Enforced Disappearance. The Convention will enter into force after the 20th ratification by a State Party. For the list of States Parties, see *Human Rights Major International Instruments, Status as at 31 May 2009* (available at www.unesco.org/human_rights/ or www.unhchr.ch).

26   As at 31 May 2009, 13 States had ratified the Inter-American Convention on the Forced Disappearance of Persons. For the list of States Parties, see *Human Rights Major International Instruments, Status as at 31 May 2009* (available at www.unesco.org/human_rights/).

27   As at 31 May 2009, 173 States were parties to the International Convention on the Elimination of All Forms of Racial Discrimination. For the list of States Parties, see *Human Rights Major International Instruments, Status as at 31 May 2009* (available at www.unesco.org/human_rights/ or www.unhchr.ch).

28   In November 1993, such a mission visited the Federal Republic of Yugoslavia (Serbia and Montenegro) to help promote dialogue for a peaceful solution of human rights problems relating to racial discrimination between Albanians and the Government in Kosovo. The Committee also sent one of its members on a mission to Croatia under the Advisory Services and Technical Assistance Programme of the United Nations Centre for Human Rights to assist the Government in the implementation of the Convention.

29   As at 31 May 2009, 50 States had made the Declaration, according to Article 14 of the Convention regarding the competence of the Committee on the Elimination of Racial Discrimination to receive and consider communications from individuals or groups. For the list of States Parties, see *Human Rights Major International Instruments, Status as at 31 May 2009* (available at www.unesco. org/human_rights/ or www.unhchr.ch).

30   On the Durban Review Conference Outcome Document, 20-24 April 2009 see www.un.org/durbanreview2009/pdf/Durban_Review_outcome_document_ En.pdf.

31   As at 31 May 2009, there were 186 States Parties to the Convention on the Elimination of All Forms of Discrimination against Women. For the list of States Parties, see *Human Rights Major International Instruments, Status as at 31 May 2009* (available at www.unesco.org/human_rights/ or www.unhchr.ch).

32   As at 31 May 2009, there were 97 States Parties to the Optional Protocol to the Convention on the Elimination of All Forms of Discrimination against Women. For the list of States Parties, see *Human Rights Major International Instruments, Status as at 31 May 2009* (available at www.unesco.org/human_rights/ or www. unhchr.ch).

33   Council of Europe, *Gender Mainstreaming,* 1998.

34   This conference was the focal point of International Women's Year.

35   Organized in the middle of the United Nations Decade for Women: Equality, Development and Peace (1976–85).

36   Adopted by Resolution 48/104 of 20 December 1993.

37   E.CN.2001/73.

38   E/CN.4.2002/83.

39   A/HRC/7/6, 2008.

40   As at 31 May 2009, there were 193 States Parties to the Convention on the Rights of the Child. For the list of States Parties, see *Human Rights Major International Instruments, Status as at 31 May 2009* (available at www.unesco. org/human_rights/ or www.unhchr.ch).

41   UNICEF was awarded the Nobel Peace Prize in 1965.

42   As at 31 May 2009, 131 States had ratified the Optional Protocol to the Convention on the Rights of the Child on the sale of children, child prostitution and child pornography. For the list of States Parties, see *Human Rights Major International Instruments, Status as at 31 May 2009* (available at www.unesco. org/human_rights/ or www.unhchr.ch).

43   As at 31 May 2009, the African Charter on the Rights and Welfare of the Child had received 45 ratifications. For the list of States Parties, see *Human Rights Major International Instruments, Status as at 31 May 2009* (available at www.unesco. org/human_rights/).

44 As at 31 May 2009, 128 States have ratified the Optional Protocol to the Convention on the Rights of the Child on the involvement of children in armed conflict. For the list of States Parties, see *Human Rights Major International Instruments, Status as at 31 May 2009* (available at www.unesco.org/human_rights/ or www.unhchr.ch).

45 A/Res/56/5.

46 SC/1379/2001.

47 S/RES/1612 (2005).

48 In one such case, Lovelace v. Canada, a Native American woman complained to the Committee that she was legally forbidden under domestic law from returning to her Indian reservation, following the dissolution of her marriage to a non-Indian. The Committee decided that there had been a violation under Article 27. In response to this decision, Canada changed its domestic law to bring it in line with international law.

49 Adopted by Resolution 47/135 of 18 December 1992.

50 General Assembly Resolution 48/138 of 20 December 1993.

51 *Study of the Rights of Persons Belonging to Ethnic, Religious and Linguistic Minorities*, prepared by Francesco Capotorti, Special Rapporteur appointed by the Subcommission at its twenty-fourth session, in 1971. Reports on Possible Ways and Means of Facilitating the Peaceful and Constructive Solution of Problems Involving Minorities, prepared by A. Eide in 1991–93.

52 This report of the United Nations Secretary-General was prepared pursuant to the statement adopted by the Summit Meeting of the Security Council on 31 January 1992, and presented in June 1992.

53 Kofi Annan, Secretary-General of the United Nations, Presentation of the Millennium Report, 3 April 2000. Available at www.un.org/millennium/sg/report/state.htm.

54 In December 1994 it was transformed into the Organization on Security and Cooperation in Europe (OSCE), comprising 56 Member States (as at May 2009).

55 As at 31 May 2009, there were 20 States Parties to the ILO Convention No. 169 concerning Indigenous and Tribal Peoples in Independent Countries. For the list of States Parties, see *Human Rights Major International Instruments, Status as at 31 May 2009* (available at www.unesco.org/human_rights/).

56 ECOSOC Resolution 2000/22.

57 Resolution 2001/57.

58 Resolution 48/163 of 21 December 1993.

59 Resolution 59/174 of 22 December 2004.

60 As at 31 May 2009, 57 States had ratified the Convention on the Rights of Persons with Disabilities and 36 States had ratified the Optional Protocol to the Convention. For the list of States Parties, see *Human Rights Major International Instruments, Status as at 31 May 2009* (available at www.unesco.org/human_rights/ or www.unhchr.ch).

61 As at 31 May 2009, 17 States were Parties to the Inter-American Convention on the Elimination of All Forms of Discrimination against Persons with Disabilities. For the list of States Parties, see *Human Rights Major International Instruments, Status as at 31 May 2009* (available at www.unesco.org/human_rights/ or www.unhchr.ch).

62 As at 31 May 2009, 141 States had ratified both the Convention relating to the Status of Refugees (entered into force in 1954) and the Protocol (entered into force in 1967). For the list of States Parties, see *Human Rights Major International Instruments, Status as at 31 May 2009* (available at www.unesco.org/human_rights/ or www.unhchr.ch). Those that had only ratified the Convention are: Madagascar, Monaco and Saint Kitts and Nevis. Those which have only ratified the Protocol were: Cape Verde, United States of America and Venezuela.

63 OAS Convention on Asylum (1928); OAS Convention on Political Asylum (1933); OAS Convention on Diplomatic Asylum (1954); OAS Convention on Territorial Asylum (1954).

64 UNHCR rendered such assistance in various countries including Afghanistan, Chad, the Democratic Republic of Congo, Pakistan and Sudan.

65 Statement by Mrs Ogata, United Nations High Commissioner for Refugees, of 5 March 1993 in the Commission on Human Rights.

66 As at 31 May 2009, there were 45 States Parties to the Convention Governing the Specific Aspects of Refugee Problems in Africa. For the list of States Parties, see *Human Rights Major International Instruments, Status as at 31 May 2009* (available at www.unesco.org/human_rights/ or www.unhchr.ch).

67 The Report to the General Assembly of the Special Representative of the Secretary-General on Internally Displaced Persons (A/56/168).

68 By 2003, no fewer than eighty-four countries had been under consideration.

69 The Group of African States has thirteen seats; the Group of Asian States has thirteen seats; the Group of Eastern European States has six; the Group of Latin American and Caribbean States has eight; and the Group of Western European and other States has seven seats in the HRC.

70 In 2008 The Working Group examined 21 reported cases under its urgent action procedure. The Working Group also reviewed 505 newly-reported cases of enforced disappearances.

71 As at 31 May 2009, the country-specific mandates were for the following States: Burundi, Cambodia, Haiti, People's Democratic Republic of Korea, Myanmar, Palestinian territories occupied since 1967, Somalia and Sudan.

72 These situations were in Equatorial Guinea, the occupied Arab territories including Palestine, and Zaire. Other situations were examined by a Working Group on Southern Africa, the Special Committee to Investigate Israeli Practices Affecting the Human Rights of the Population of the Occupied Arab Territories and the Committee on the Exercise of the Inalienable Rights of the Palestinian People.

73 For example, in 1994, there were six such officers located in Zagreb (Croatia) in the service of the Special Rapporteur on the former Yugoslavia.

74 UN Press Release, 12 March 2007, available at www.un.org/apps/news/story.asp?NewsID=21834&Cr=rights&Cr1=council.

75 Human Rights Council Resolution, A/HRC/RES/5/1, 18 June 2007.

76 General Assembly Resolution 60/251, 16 March 2006.

77 1. Convention for the Amelioration of the Condition of the Wounded and Sick in Armed Forces in the Field; 2. Convention for the Amelioration of the Condition of the Wounded, Sick, and Shipwrecked Members of Armed Forces at Sea; 3. Convention Relative to the Treatment of Prisoners of War; and 4. Convention Relative to the Protection of Civilian Persons in Time of War. All four Conventions were adopted on 12 August 1949 and entered into force on 21 October 1950.

78   The Additional Protocol I to the Geneva Conventions entered into force on 7 December 1978 and as of 31 May 2009, 168 States were parties to it. For the list of States Parties, see *Human Rights Major International Instruments, Status as at 31 May 2009* (available at www.unesco.org/human_rights/).

79   The Additional Protocol II to the Geneva Conventions entered into force on 7 December 1978 and as of 31 May 2009, 164 States were parties to it. For the list of States Parties, see *Human Rights Major International Instruments, Status as at 31 May 2009* (available at www.unesco.org/human_rights/).

80   Some experts consider the UNESCO Convention for the Protection of Cultural Property in the Event of Armed Conflict, with Regulations for the Execution of the Convention, as well as the Protocol to the Convention and the Conference Resolutions (1954), to form part of humanitarian law.

81   Founded in 1863, the International Committee of the Red Cross and the Federation of Red Cross and Red Crescent Societies form, with the National Red Cross and Red Crescent Societies, the International Red Cross and Red Crescent Movement. The ICRC was awarded the Nobel Peace Prize in 1917, 1944 and 1963.

82   The full title is The International Tribunal for the Prosecution of Persons Responsible for Serious Violations of International Humanitarian Law.

83   In a letter dated 14 May 2009 the President of the ICTR reported to the Security Council that the workload of the Court during 2009 will not make it possible for the Court to conclude its proceedings according to the Completion Strategy. See UN Doc s/2009/247, 14 May 2009 available at http://69.94.11.53/ENGLISH/completionstrat/s-2009-247e.pdf.

84   Security Council Resolution 1350, August 2000.

85   A Special Working Group on the Crime of Aggression was established in 2002 by the Assembly of States Parties to continue discussions on the definition, elements and jurisdictional conditions of the Crime of Aggression. As of May 2008, when the last report of the Working Group was issued, there has not been any working definition on the crime of aggression. Available on http://www.iccnow.org/?mod=aggression&lang=en.

86   As at 31 May 2009, the Court had opened investigations into four situations: Northern Uganda, Democratic republic of Congo, Central African Republic and Darfur (Sudan).

87   Vienna Declaration and Programme of Action, para. 18.

88   High Commissioners Strategic Management Plan 2008-2009, available at http://www.ohchr.org/Documents/Press/SMP2008-2009.pdf.

89   The ninth Treaty Body is to be established upon the entry into force of the Convention for the Protection of All Persons from Enforced Disappearance. As at 31 May 2009, the relevant Convention had not yet entered into force.

90   The Voluntary Fund for Victims of Torture, the Voluntary Trust Fund on Contemporary Forms of Slavery and the Voluntary Fund on Indigenous Populations are administered by the Secretary General. The Voluntary Fund for Technical Cooperation in the Field of Human Rights is administered by OHCHR.

91   Such offices have been established, for example, in Cambodia, Colombia, Croatia, Bosnia and Herzegovina, Democratic Republic of Congo, and the Federal Republic of Yugoslavia.

92   See 2005 World Summit Outcome Document, General Assembly Resolution A/RES/60/1, 24 October 2005.

93   See 2005 World Summit Outcome Document, General Assembly Resolution A/RES/60/1, 24 October 2005.

94	The Recommendation concerning the Status of the Artist (1980), the Universal Copyright Convention (1952, revised in 1971) and the Recommendation on the Status of Scientific Researchers (1974).
95	As at 31 May 2009, 95 States were Parties to the UNESCO Convention against Discrimination in Education. For the list of States Parties, see *Human Rights Major International Instruments, Status as at 31 May 2009* (available at www.unesco.org/human_rights/ or www.unhchr.ch).
96	The UNESCO Protocol Instituting a Conciliation and Good Offices Commission to be Responsible for Seeking the Settlement of any Disputes which may Arise between States Parties to the Convention against Discrimination in Education, adopted in 1962, entered into force in 1968. By the end of May 2009, 34 States were parties to this Protocol. For the list of States Parties, see *Human Rights Major International Instruments, Status as at 31 May 2009* (available at www.unesco.org/human_rights/ or www.unhchr.ch).
97	162 EX/Decision 3.2.2.
98	157 EX/Decision 6.3.
99	As provided by Article 23, the Intergovernmental Committee of the Convention on the Protection and Promotion of the Diversity of Cultural Expressions was established when the number of Parties exceeded 50. The Committee is composed of representatives of 24 States Parties to the Convention, 'elected for a term of four years by the Conference of Parties'. More information on the Intergovernmental Committee is available on the UNESCO Official Website: www.unesco.org.
100	As at 31 May 2009, 98 States and the European Community had ratified the Convention on the Protection and Promotion of the Diversity of Cultural Expressions. For the names of States Parties, see *Human Rights Major International Instruments, Status as at 31 May 2009* (available at www.unesco.org/human_rights/).
101	UNESCO Rules of Procedure of the Executive Board, 2005 edition, available at http://unesdoc.unesco.org/images/0013/001390/139080e.pdf 9.
102	ILO was awarded the Nobel Peace Prize in 1969.
103	On the Report of the World Commission on the Social Dimension of Globalization see www.ilo.org/fairglobalization/report/lang--en/index.htm.
104	The Decent Work Agenda is a concept elaborated in the ILO Framework and is based on employment, social protection, social dialogue and tripartism, and fundamental principles and rights at work. For more information on the concept see http://www.ilo.org/global/About_the_ILO/Media_and_public_information/Press_releases/lang--en/WCMS_094186/index.htm.
105	Albania, Andorra, Armenia, Austria, Azerbaidjan, Belgium, Bosnia and Herzegovina, Bulgaria, Croatia, Cyprus, Czech Republic, Denmark, Estonia, Finland, France, Georgia, Germany, Greece, Hungary, Iceland, Ireland, Italy, Latvia, Liechtenstein, Lithuania, Luxembourg, Malta, Monaco, Montenegro, Netherlands, Norway, Poland, Portugal, Republic of Moldova, Romania, Russian Federation, San Marino, Serbia, Slovak Republic, Slovenia, Spain, Sweden, Switzerland, the former Yugoslav Republic of Macedonia, Turkey, Ukraine, and the United Kingdom.
106	As at 31 May 2009, 46 States had ratified the Protocol No 14 to the Convention for the Protection of Human Rights and Fundamental Freedoms Amending the Control System of the Convention. For the list of States Parties, see *Human Rights Major International Instruments, Status as at 31 May 2009* (available at www.unesco.org/human_rights/ or www.unhchr.ch).

On 12 May 2009, Protocol No. 14bis to the European Convention for the Protection of Human rights and fundamental freedoms was adopted, containing technical arrangements on the functioning of the Court.

107　As at 31 May 2009, there were 27 States Parties to the European Social Charter and 27 States Parties to the revised European Social Charter. For the list of States Parties, see *Human Rights Major International Instruments, Status as at 31 May 2009* (available at www.unesco.org/human_rights/ or www.unhchr.ch).

108　The Group of Experts on Action against Trafficking in Human Beings (GRETA) held its first meeting in February 2009. See http://www.coe.int/t/dghl/monitoring/trafficking/default_en.asp.

109　On the establishment of the financial instrument for the promotion of democracy and human rights in the world (Regulation (EC) No 1889/2006 of the European Parliament and of the Council of 20 December 2006) see http://eur-lex.europa.eu/smartapi/cgi/sga_doc?smartapi!celexplus!prod!DocNumber&lg=en &type_doc=Regulation&an_doc=2006&nu_doc=1889.

110　European Union, Council of the EU, Mainstreaming human rights across CFSP and other EU policies, Brussels, 7 June 2006 (10076/06), available at http://www.consilium.europa.eu/ueDocs/cms_Data/docs/hr/news66.pdf .

111　As at 31 May 2009, 53 States had ratified the Constitutive Act of the African Union. For the list of States Parties, see *Human Rights Major International Instruments, Status as at 31 May 2009* (available at www.unesco.org/human_rights/ or www.unhchr.ch).

112　As at 31 May 2009, Ethiopia and Mauritania had ratified the African Charter on Democracy, Elections and Governance. See *Human Rights Major International Instruments, Status as at 31 May 2009* (available at www.unesco.org/human_rights/ or www.unhchr.ch).

113　As at 31 May 2009, 13 States had ratified the African Youth Charter. For the list of States Parties, see *Human Rights Major International Instruments, Status as at 31 May 2009* (available at www.unesco.org/human_rights/ or www.unhchr.ch).

114　As at 31 May 2009, the Protocol had not yet entered into force. See www.africa-union.org/root/AU/Documents/Treaties/text/Protocol%20on%20the%20 Merged%20Court%20-%20EN.pdf.

115　For more details, see www.achpr.org.

116　This has only been done in one instance, in 1994, when a violation was found against Malawi.

117　The OAS was created in 1890 under the name of the International Union of American Republics and changed its name to Organization of American States in 1948.

118　By 31 May 2009, 24 States had ratified the American Convention on Human Rights. For the list of States Parties, see *Human Rights Major International Instruments, Status as at 31 May 2009* (available at www.unesco.org/human_rights/).

119　For the list of States Parties, see *Human Rights Major International Instruments, Status as at 31 May 2009* (available at www.unesco.org/human_rights/).

120　There were thirty-five participating States in 1975. As at 31 May 2009, there are 56 Participating States to the OSCE See www.osce.org.

121　The twenty-two Member States of the League of Arab States are: Jordan, United Arab Emirates, Bahrain, Tunisia, Algeria, Djibouti, Saudi Arabia, Sudan, Syrian Arab Republic, Somalia, Iraq, Oman, Palestine, Qatar, Comoros, Kuwait, Lebanon, Libyan Arab Jamahiriya, Egypt, Morocco, Mauritania and Yemen.

122   For more information see http://www.un.org/esa/coordination/ngo/ (last checked on 31 January 2009).

123   See the Vienna Declaration and Programme of Action (para. 38 of the Declaration).

124   Declaration of Principles, United Nations Conference on Environment and Development, Rio de Janeiro, 3-14 June 1992; Copenhagen Declaration on Social Development and Programme of Action, March 1995.

125   Declaration of Principles, United Nations Conference on Environment and Development, Rio de Janeiro, 3-14 June 1992.

126   Doc. A/51/506/Add. 1, 12 December 1996, para. 2.

127   Adopted by the International Congress on Education for Human Rights and Democracy convened in Montreal (Canada) from 8 to 11 March 1993, by UNESCO and the United Nations Centre for Human Rights, in collaboration with the Canadian Commission for UNESCO.

128   Report of the United Nations High Commisssioner for Human Rights on the mid-term global evaluation of the progress made towards the achievement of the objectives of the United Nations Decade for Human Rights Education (1995-2004), A/55/360, 7 September 2000, http://daccessdds.un.org/doc/UNDOC/GEN/N00/640/37/PDF/N0064037.pdf?OpenElement.

129   The Declaration was adopted by the 44th session of the International Conference on Education, Geneva, Switzerland, 1994 and the Integrated Framework was adopted by the 28th session of UNESCO's General Conference, Paris, France, 1995.

130   Europe (Turku, Finland, 1997), Africa (Dakar, Senegal, 1998), Asia and the Pacific (Pune, India, 1999) and Arab States (Rabat, Morocco, 1999), Latin America and the Caribbean (Mexico City, Mexico, 2001.

131   See UNESCO Strategy on Human Rights 2003, available at http://unesdoc. unesco.org/images/0014/001457/145734e.pdf.

132   For more information on this subject see http://portal.unesco.org/education/en/ ev.php-URL_ID=57292&URL_DO=DO_TOPIC&URL_SECTION=201. html.

133   UN Doc. A/54/1 (1999) para. 275.

134   General Assembly Resolution A/RES/53/202, 1998.

135   Human Rights Council, Resolution A/HRC/S-10/L.1, 23 February 2009.

136   General Assembly Resolution A/RES/55/2 or A/55/L.2, 2000.

137   The Millenium Development Goals Report 2008, United Nations New York 2008, available at http://www.un.org/millenniumgoals/pdf/The%20Millennium%20 Development%20Goals%20Report%202008.pdf.

138   General Assembly Resolution of 4 December 1986, A/RES/41/28.

139   Report of the Secretary-General, 'Renewing the United Nations: A Programme for Reform', A/51/950, 1997.

140   Claiming the Millennium Development Goals: A Human rights Approach, 2008, available at www.ohchr.org/Documents/Publications/Claiming_MDGs_ en.pdf.

141   Joint Statement by UN High Commissioner for Human Rights, Secretary General of the Council of Europe and the Director of the OSCE Office for Democratic Institutions and Human Rights, 29 November 2001.

142   General Assembly Resolution 48/126 of 20 December 1993.

143 The Protocol enters into force between the States which ratify or accede to it when they deposit their respective instruments of ratification or accession (Article 4) As of 31 May 2009, 11 States have ratified the Protocol. For the list of States Parties see: *Human Rights Major International Instruments, Status as at 31 May 2009* (available at www.unesco.org/human_rights/).

144 As of 31 May 2009, 46 States have ratified the Protocol No. 6 to the Convention for the Protection of Human Rights and Fundamental Freedoms concerning the Abolition of the Death Penalty. For the list of States Parties see: *Human Rights Major International Instruments, Status as at 31 May 2009* (available at www. unesco.org/human_rights/).

145 The Supplementary Convention on the Abolition of Slavery, the Slave Trade and Institutions and Practices Similar to Slavery entered into force on 30 April 1957 and as at 31 May 2009 123 States were Parties to it. For the list of States Parties, see *Human Rights Major International Instruments, Status as at 31 May 2009* (available at www.unesco.org/human_rights/ or www.unhchr.ch).

146 The Convention on the Suppression of the Traffic in Persons and of the Exploitation of the Prostitution of Others entered into force in 1951. As at 31 May 2009 81 States were Parties to it. For the list of States Parties, see *Human Rights Major International Instruments, Status as at 31 May 2009* (available at www.unesco. org/human_rights/ or www.unhchr.ch).

147 The Basic Principles were adopted by the Seventh United Nations Congress on the Prevention of Crime and the Treatment of Offenders (Milan, Italy, 26 August–6 September 1985).

148 The Convention on the Reduction of Statelessness entered into force in 1975. As at 31 May 2009, 36 States were Parties to it. For the list of States Parties, see *Human Rights Major International Instruments, Status as at 31 May 2009* (available at www.unesco.org/human_rights/ or www.unhchr.ch).

149 The Convention on the Consent to Marriage, Minimum Age for Marriage and Registration of Marriages entered into force in 1964 and as at 31 May 2009, 54 States were Parties to it. For the list of States Parties, see *Human Rights Major International Instruments, Status as at 31 May 2009* (available at www.unesco. org/human_rights/ or www.unhchr.ch).

150 For example, the ILO Convention (No. 87) concerning Freedom of Association and Protection of the Right to Organize (adopted in 1948 and entered into force in 1950) had, as at 31 May 2009, been ratified by 149 States, while the ILO Convention (No. 151) concerning Protection of the Right to Organize and Procedures for Determining Conditions of Employment in the Public Service (adopted in 1978 and entered into force in 1981) had only been ratified by 44. The ILO Convention (No. 98) concerning the Application of the Principles of the Right to Organize and Bargain Collectively (adopted in 1949 and entering into force in 1951) had the largest number of States Parties – 159 States – as of 31 May 2009. For the list of States Parties, see *Human Rights Major International Instruments, Status as at 31 May 2009* (available at www.unesco. org/human_rights/ or www.unhchr.ch).

151 General Assembly Resolution 55/199 of 20 December 2000.

152 Document A/.2/57/L83.

Abbreviations

ACHPR	African Commission on Human and Peoples' Rights
ALECSO	Arab League Educational, Cultural and Scientific Organization
ASEAN	Association of Southeast Asian Nations
AHRB	ASEAN Human Rights Body
AU	African Union
CAAC	Security Council Working Group on Children and Armed Conflict (UN)
CAT	Committee against Torture
CEART	Committee of Experts on the Application of the Recommendations concerning Teaching Personnel
CEDAW	Committee on the Elimination of Discrimination Against Women
CERD	Committee on the Elimination of Racial Discrimination
CESCR	Committee on Economic, Social and Cultural Rights
CoE	Council of Europe
CPT	European Committee for the Prevention of Torture
CRC	Committee on the Rights of the Child
CSCE	Conference on Security and Cooperation in Europe
EC	European Community
ECHR	European Court of Human Rights
ECOSOC	European and Social Council
ECRE	European Commission on Racial Equality
ECRI	European Commission against Racism and Intolerance
ECSR	European Committee of Social Rights
ESCAP	Economic and Social Commission for Asia and the Pacific
ESDP	European Security and Defence Policy (EU)
EU	European Union
FAO	Food and Agriculture Organization of the United Nations
GA	General Assembly (UN)

GRETA	Group of Experts on Action against Trafficking in Human Beings (CoE)
HABITAT	UN Centre for Human Settlements
HCNM	High Commissioner on Natinal Minorities (OSCE)
HLP	High Level Panel on the Establishment of an ASEAN human rights body
HRBA	Human Rights Based Approach
HRC	Human Rights Committee / Human Rights Council
HRE	Human Rights Education
IBC	International Bioethics Committee (UNESCO)
ICC	International Criminal Court (UN)/ International Coordinating Committee of National Institutions for the Promotion and Protection of Human Rights
ICCPR	International Covenant on Civil and Political Rights
ICESCR	International Covenant on Economic, Social and Cultural Rights
ICJ	International Court of Justice
ICRC	International Committee of the Red Cross
ICTR	International Criminal Tribunal for Rwanda
ICTY	International Criminal Tribunal for the Former Yugoslavia
IDPs	Internally displaced persons
ILO	International Labour Organization
IMF	International Monetary Fund
IOM	International Organization for Migration
IPEC	International Programme for the Elimination of Child Labour
IRO	International Refugee Organization
MRM	Monitoring and Reporting Mechanism of the Security Council on Children and Armed Conflict (UN)
NEPAD	New Partnership for Africa's Development
NGOs	Non-governmental organizations
NHRIs	National Human Rights Institutions
OAS	Organization of American States
OAU	Organization of African Unity
ODIHR	Office for Democratic Institutions and Human Rights (OSCE)

OECD	Organisation for Economic Co-operation and Development
OHCHR	Office of the United Nations High Commissioner for Human Rights
OSCE	Organisation for Security and Co-operation in Europe
POW	Prisoner of war
TEC	Treaty establishing the European Community
TEU	Treaty on European Union
TNC	Transnational Corporations
UDHR	Universal Declaration of Human Rights
UN	United Nations
UNAIDS	United Nations Programme on HIV/AIDS
UNDP	United Nations Development Programme
UNESCO	United Nations Educational, Scientific and Cultural Organization
UNHCR	United Nations High Commissioner for Refugees
UNICEF	United Nations Children's Fund
UNIDO	United Nations Industrial Development Organization
UNIFEM	United Nations Development Fund for Women
UNPFII	United Nations Permanent Forum on Indigenous Issues
UPR	Universal Periodic Review (UN)
VDPA	Vienna Declaration and Programme of Action
WCAR	World Conference against Racism, Racial Discrimination, Xenophobia and Related Intolerance
WFP	World Food Programme
WHO	World Health Organization
WIPO	World Intellectual Property Organization
WSSD	World Summit for Sustainable Development
WTO	World Trade Organization

NOTES

NOTES

NOTES

NOTES

NOTES

NOTES